SKYSCRAPER

Timothy S. Nurse

To my guardian angel Tamika
To my sheros Verna, Ellen, and Sonya
To my daily inspiration Emerald and Elivia
To my lifetime reservoir Diamond

Table of Contents

Introduction

Who doesn't want more from their career? We all do! Regardless of your field, the ideal career path is a direct route: getting paid extremely well for doing a job you deeply enjoy. However, for many professionals in their current roles, that dream scenario can seem miles away. As the years go by without changing your approach to your career, you probably feel even farther from your ideal career, and the chances of finding fulfillment may appear to be dwindling.

If you were anything like me when I was in school, you probably had a clear career in mind and envisioned yourself in a position of power. But once you entered the "real world," your career path likely took on a life of its own. And now, here you are — unhappy and constantly pondering the "what ifs" and "should haves," trying to figure out where you fit in corporate America. Rest assured, you're not alone. Many successful professionals, including myself, have spent time in unfulfilling jobs. There was a time when I experienced daily anxiety, not only because my corporate job sucked, but also because I had no clue if I had chosen the right profession, what a successful career truly looked like, or where I should be working within a corporation. I felt stuck. But then, I had an epiphany that answered those questions and led me to a formula that transformed my sucky job into a career I genuinely enjoy.

In its simplest form, this formula for a more fulfilling career path consists of two ingredients: clear purpose and meaningful connections. When I applied this formula during my time as an Assistant Vice President, the first ingredient, clear purpose, granted me freedom. It's liberating to know how the tasks I complete each day align with where I intend to work in the future. The second ingredient, meaningful connections, provides me with access to executive leaders who can assist me in securing a lucrative career path and job security. The professional relationships I nurtured over the years give me access to hundreds of leaders. I can instantly reach out to any of them to discuss anything, from a fun family weekend to seeking advice on my next career move. These connections include senior vice presidents, directors, and executives from ten of the Fortune 100 companies. The stronger my relationship with these leaders, the more they trust me and are willing to help me secure a lucrative job if I ever need to make a professional change. After I put this formula into action, I landed a career that I love, built connections with powerful people, and secured a higher income.

I couldn't keep this method to success to myself. When I shared it with colleagues, to my surprise, those who took just a few of the steps saw positive changes in their careers. Some experienced happiness in their work for the first time, some gained increased optimism about their career decisions, others established professional relationships with leaders in their industry, and some even summoned the courage to make the career moves they always wanted to make. I knew I was onto something.

As a result, my colleagues began referring their mentees to me. My schedule quickly filled up with thirty-minute coffee chats with employees yearning for strategies to advance their careers. However, I soon realized that most people listened to my process, understood how the formula works, desired outstanding results, but failed to apply any of the actual steps.

Time and time again, even months after our conversations, I witnessed individuals who didn't apply the formula ending up in another job they disliked, longing for more fulfillment at work. There was a need for increased accountability and a breakdown of the formula into smaller actionable activities.

This realization led me to start a career coaching business called *Careers in Action LLC®* and create the *Career Accelerator Program*, an 8-session accountability program designed to teach employees how to achieve the careers they genuinely desire. We take my career-building formula, known as the *Skyscraper Method*, and break it down into manageable steps. The program's primary objective is to empower participants to take control of their career paths and build the right network. Through carefully crafted activities, we uncover any issues in their current career journey, establish career goals aligned with their professional passion, and help them overcome networking fears. The program demonstrates effective strategies for planning one's career and network in a way that enables productive conversations, just as they would with peers.

The initial version of the Career Accelerator Program was a pilot, and despite a few setbacks, I witnessed widespread success with the method. I received tons of feedback, with participants sharing which strategies worked well for them and which ones didn't. I made adjustments, keeping the best parts of the method and incorporating them into what is presented in this book. The results have been consistently amazing.

To my delight, the Career Accelerator Program became a resounding success. Participants experienced eye-opening realizations about their career paths. They shifted their focus from career goals handed down by employers to self-developed goals that resonated with their passions. Overall, they felt a greater sense of control over their career choices, proactively mapping their journey instead of merely reacting to the one imposed on them.

During sessions, program participants shared stories of receiving job offers without even having to interview and finding roles they absolutely love in their respective industries. The *Skyscraper Method* empowered participants to actively pursue their career goals rather than passively waiting for opportunities to arise. The networking tools and techniques provided in the program helped them confidently "break the ice" with executives, where they would have otherwise felt nervous. Participants gained valuable perspective on their career choices and identified areas of improvement that they had previously overlooked. Once they started following the actionable steps outlined in the *Skyscraper Method*, they noticed an immediate shift in career opportunities.

A survey conducted with over 100 participants, about 18 months after completing the program, revealed impressive statistics: 83% received a promotion, 72% switched to a different role that they genuinely enjoyed, and 85% established multiple new professional relationships with business leaders. Moreover, the post-program survey showed that employees experienced an average base salary increase of 30%. They were now working with greater purpose, benefiting from more mentors, and earning more money.

If you desire similar results for your career, then you've chosen the right book. *Skyscraper: A Proven Method to Build Your Dream Career* is the comprehensive guide you need to accelerate your career and tap into the right network. This book details the formula and strategies I discussed earlier, and much more. If you're tired of feeling frustrated and ready to make a change in your career path today — not next week or next month — then join the Skyscraper family and elevate your career to new heights.

What is this book about?

Well, let me tell you about the *"Skyscraper method"*. This book offers professionals, both new and experienced, a fresh perspective on building a successful career. Instead of focusing solely on a predetermined career path, I emphasize a 'career building' mindset that guides individuals to define their purpose and cultivate meaningful relationships. My approach is tactical, providing a roadmap for professionals who feel stuck, overworked, and underpaid, to get on the path towards success, fulfillment, and the *skyscraper* career they desire.

Moreover, by engaging the *Skyscraper* methodology, you'll embark on a journey of self-reflection to identify your unique advantage. It could be your nationality, background, physical attributes, or technical skill set. This encourages you to craft a personal mission statement that uncovers what sets you apart from your colleagues or a pool of applicants. Through networking,developing professional relationships, and delivering exceptional work, you'll acquire tools to showcase your individuality. As you build your career, you should bring your whole self to work and proudly share these aspects with the world, free from shame or fear.

At the very least, by the time you reach the end of this book, you'll have a better understanding that everyone faces challenges in their career-building journey. Even I have had my fair share of struggles. If this book does nothing else but help you recognize the value of strategizing each step of your career, I would consider it a success. However, my hope is that it goes far beyond that, and you apply the strategies I've shared to create lasting changes in your career.

This book is designed to give you a taste of what it would be like to have me as your career coach, with an extra seasoning of the Career Accelerator Program. It is divided into eight phases, each exploring a key topic, the underlying strategies for that topic, and how to apply them to your own career journey. These topics and strategies are interconnected, with each chapter preparing you for the next step in your career-building process.

Who is this book for?

Well, let me break it down for you. *Skyscraper* is a guide tailored to ambitious early-career professionals who want to establish a strong foundation, as well as mid-career professionals who feel like their careers have hit a roadblock and are unhappy with their daily work routine. The tips and strategies shared in this book are specifically designed to be applied within a traditional corporate structure, where decisions are made by c-suite leaders (such as the Chief Executive Officer and Chief Operations Officer) and employees follow a chain of command.

To all you ambitious early-career professionals who are relatively new to corporate America and crave authenticity, direct communication, and relevance from your employer, this book is for you. Finding a job may be easy, but discovering a meaningful career can be challenging. Utilize this book as a guide to assemble a team of career advisors who can help you navigate potential pitfalls. It is possible to leave your mark on corporate America quickly. You can aim for your dream position within a specific corporation and achieve it early on. The first step to constructing a *skyscraper* is to delve deep within yourself. This introspection will provide clarity on your professional passions, ultimately guiding you towards the best possible career path(s).

And to all frustrated mid-career professionals who have yet to find that job that truly excites you after years of working in corporate America, it might be time for a career change. If you feel that change is necessary, it's likely long overdue. However, let's approach it strategically. This book will inspire you to position yourself correctly for a career shift that can transform your life— and maybe even change the world. If you don't take action now, you'll regret not investing in yourself when you wake up ten years from now, still feeling the same dissatisfaction. Embrace the *"Skyscraper Method"* and make a calculated career move that propels you into a fulfilling path rather than one you dread. You have the ability to do it! Don't hesitate! The time to level up is NOW! Let's go!

I've been in both of these situations. I understand the conflicting emotions of excitement upon graduation with aspirations of conquering the world, mixed with the fear of the unknown challenges that await in the "real world." I also know the frustration and dissatisfaction of being in a role that doesn't align with your true self, even when everything appears perfect from the outside. It's a miserable feeling. That's precisely why

I wrote this book. I've got you covered with tested tools and strategies on these pages that will help you find career satisfaction and personal fulfillment.

Job vs.Career

Understanding the distinction between a job and a career is crucial when diving into this book. The skills and strategies you'll acquire here are most effective for those who frequently jump from one job to another. It's essential to grasp this distinction early on, so you don't waste your time and effort attempting to build a career within the confines of a job environment.

Now, how can you differentiate between a job and a career? Sure, you can consult a dictionary or do a quick Google search for definitions, but let me offer you some straightforward ways to distinguish the two. A job often feels like a monotonous grind, while a career is an ongoing journey of growth and development. Jobs tend to be short-term, while careers are built for the long haul. Employees in a job often do the bare minimum, lacking care or motivation. Conversely, individuals on a career path have a strong drive to continually improve and expand both professionally and personally. When you have a job, you simply exchange your time for money. However, with a career, you not only earn a living but also accumulate valuable experiences that often come with higher compensation as you progress and evolve.

Take a moment now to reflect on your own occupation. Are you merely in a job, or are you actively constructing a fulfilling career?

How can you get the most from reading this book?

To extract the maximum value from *Skyscraper*, I highly recommend reading it not once, but twice. Why? Well, on your initial pass, devour the book from cover to cover, allowing the blueprint to imprint itself deep within your subconscious. Then, on your second read, savor each chapter, take your time to internalize the lessons and actively engage with the exercises provided. By immersing yourself in this deliberate and reflective process, you will emerge with a powerful career navigation system that empowers you to leverage your corporate connections and construct the ideal path for your career aspirations.

Here's one last piece of advice: Approach the book with an open mind as you reflect on your own journey and diligently complete the assignments. And remember, there's no need to delay. Don't wait for the perfect moment to take action. The time to embark on your career transformation is now. Seize the opportunity and make that change!

Where did the term Skyscraper come from?

Well, let's embark on a journey into the realm of imagination. Ever since I was a young child, I possessed a vivid and boundless imagination. I would often find myself lost in my thoughts, daydreaming about my favorite cartoons like Tiny Toon Adventures, X-Men, and Transformers. In the realms of my mind, I would bring these animated characters to life and hang out with them. Picture this: playing solitaire with

Optimus Prime and engaging in spirited spades games with the lively crew from Animaniacs. While I controlled all the moves, it was an absolute blast for me. You see, my mother, a hardworking single parent, had to take extra shifts, and my older sister was deeply immersed in her fashion ventures. So, to keep myself occupied and away from any negative influences, I would spend my after-school hours at home, unleashing my imagination. And let me tell you, my ace, the X-men leader Wolverine, was there for me when I struggled in 8th-grade English. My imagination served as a playful outlet back then, and to this day, it continues to grant me the ability to perceive things from unique perspectives.

With that same imaginative lens, I perceive each client's career journey as a bustling construction site. As we delve into the implementation of the *Skyscraper Method*, in the depths of my mind's eye, we step into a vibrant construction zone, ready to revamp and remodel an existing structure. Now, some structures require more work than others, and each phase of the method is intrinsically linked to enhancing that very structure. Allow me to paint you a picture: as we identify specific opportunities for career improvement, I envision us donning hard hats, diligently inspecting the current blueprint for any potential issues. The process of unearthing the jobs that ignite your deepest passions is akin to digging deep into the soil, seeking a solid foundation. And when you begin networking with a multitude of influential leaders, skillfully conveying your work history and career aspirations, my mind's eye envisions this growing network of leaders as the building rises higher, level by level. And thus, I reached the conclusion that since there is no structure taller than a skyscraper, the name "*Skyscraper Method*" resonates perfectly.

So, my friends, embrace your imagination, for it holds the power to transform your career journey. Let the *Skyscraper Method* guide you as you construct a solid foundation, expand your network, and reach towering heights of success. It's time to unleash your creative spirit and build a career that stands tall among the rest.

Things to Keep in Mind

There are a few key phrases and acronyms that I want to define right off the bat.

1. Career in Action Activity

As you progress through the book, you'll come across various activities that I strongly urge you to complete. These assignments serve a collective purpose: to empower you to take control of your career. They assist you in defining your desires in a role and help you prepare the necessary self-marketing tools and talking points for those opportune networking moments. Engaging in these activities is an excellent way to break free from a rut and discover fresh solutions to old problems. I encourage you to embrace each activity and give it your all, as they lay the foundation for your career transformation.

2. CCC Rule

CCC stands for Clear, Correct, Concise. It's a helpful acronym to bear in mind when communicating with colleagues, mentors, or executives in a corporate setting. It also applies when completing the Career in Action activities.

Let's explore each word and understand why it serves as a fundamental rule for professional communication:

CLEAR – It's crucial to ensure that your communication, whether written or spoken, is crystal clear. This holds immense importance, particularly in professional environments. Sending an email with no punctuation or a PowerPoint deck with an unclear request won't leave a favorable impression on an executive. Here are a few tips to enhance clarity in your communications: read your written words aloud before sending an email and have a trusted colleague review your presentations or briefs to identify any ambiguous language or phrasing. The goal is to deliver messages that are unambiguous and interpreted exactly as you intended.

CORRECT – Few things are more embarrassing than having an executive point out a spelling mistake during your presentation. It's not the lasting impression you want to leave on a group of executives! Cultivate the habit of double and triple checking your work. This applies to spelling errors as well as inaccuracies in your research. Put in the necessary effort beforehand to ensure that your work is impeccable.

CONCISE – Keep it short and simple, just like the definition of 'concise.' Use the fewest words possible to convey your ideas. Excessive words without substance can confuse readers, resulting in a vague message. In the corporate world, wordy writing in emails, resumes, or proposals dilutes the impact. Concise writing is more memorable and holds the reader's attention. Writing concisely requires effort, but every word should make a lasting impact on your reader.

3. Bruce Lee Mentality

Bruce Lee, the renowned martial artist and actor from Hong Kong, serves as an inspiration in many aspects of my life. I was introduced to his remarkable journey through the biopic movie "Dragon: A Bruce Lee Story" when I was around 11 years old. I instantly fell in love with everything associated with Bruce Lee, from Kung Fu to Nunchucks and China. His life story, depicted in multiple movies, was incredibly inspiring. Bruce Lee was not only a physical force but also a philosophical thinker, with numerous quotes that resonate even today.

One quote, in particular, changed my perspective: "Apply what's useful, discard what's not, and add what's uniquely your own." I embrace this motto when receiving advice from others, and I strongly encourage you to do the same. This principle applies not only while reading this book but also when considering advice from any source. Every reader will derive different takeaways from the *Skyscraper Method*. Some tips may be familiar, while others may be entirely new. However, by adopting the "Bruce Lee mentality" and infusing your unique perspective, your individuality will shine through.

As you get further into this book, it becomes crucial to tailor the advice to suit your specific needs rather than blindly adhering to everything within its pages. Ensure that the information you absorb is applicable to your situation. Remove anything that doesn't align, and then add your own style and flavor. The Bruce Lee Mentality should always be present in your mind as you read and navigate through life. Whether the advice comes from your boss, your pastor, your family, or your life partner, there will always be elements you'll need to adapt and transform to make it truly your own.

4. Terms

Influencer: A professional who possesses the power to reshape the trajectory of your career as a mentor or business leader with a vested interest in your success.

Clients: Professionals who invest in my *Careers in Action®* career coaching services, which encompass a wide range of offerings, including but not limited to professional branding, interview preparation, resume review, networking action plan, salary negotiation, and career development.

5. Take Your Time

While it is possible to devour this entire book in a single weekend, I urge you not to do so. Instead, I guide my clients to complete the activities and observe how each one shapes their perspective on their career journey. I suggest you adopt the same approach. Give yourself ample time to engage in the practical exercises and reflect on their impact. Choose one strategy from each chapter that resonates most with your current situation, rather than overwhelming yourself by attempting ten new strategies all at once. Afterward, I would love to hear about your results. Seriously, feel free to email me at tsncareers@ gmail.com with the subject line "Career in Action Activity." Your feedback is invaluable to me.

Let's get after it! Your First Assignment

Career in Action Activity: List Opportunity Area(s)

Choose one thing that you want to change about your career today. If you have more than one please list them out. Then meet me in Chapter 1, where we'll investigate what the *skyscraper method* is and learn how to apply it to change the future of your career.

Chapter 1:
The *Skyscraper Method*

Skyscraper Method

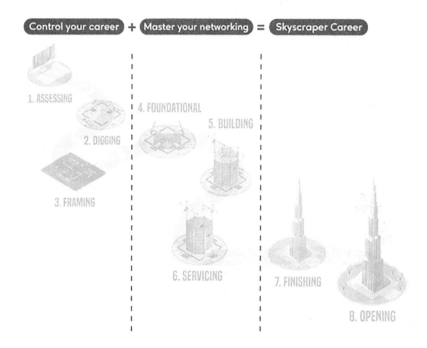

What is the *Skyscraper Method*?

Today, I want to introduce you to a game-changing formula that has transformed my own career and can do the same for you. It's called the *Skyscraper method*, a unique approach that combines networking and a focus on aligning your passion with your profession. So, let's explore this uncommon career strategy that can fast-track your success.

The *Skyscraper Method* empowers you to lift your head up, connect with others, envision your dream job, and navigate towards it with purpose. It's all about taking full ownership of your career and deepening your work relationships in a highly efficient manner. By applying this method effectively, you could witness remarkable career growth and experience title changes and expanded scopes within as little as three months.

Now, let's address the traditional notion of a career path as a linear journey that leads to a corner office and a personal assistant. I'm here to tell you that it's nothing more than a fairy tale. This book is for those who have realized the limitations of the "Heads down, Hard Work" (HDHW) approach. You've probably noticed that despite your efforts, achievements, promotions, and overall fulfillment don't always align. That's where the *Skyscraper Method* comes in.

To break through to the next level of your career, you need to embrace a "head up, hard work" (HUHW) approach that revolves around developing and nurturing meaningful relationships. By consistently applying this approach, you'll shatter the limitation on how far you can advance in your career. No matter how high you climb the corporate ladder, there will always be new connections that can teach you, amplify your impact, and increase your value. The potential of the HUHW approach is limitless.

During my 20-plus years in corporate America, I've observed the following about the HDHW approach: Hard work alone isn't enough to catch a hiring manager's attention for promotions. HDHW employees often fail to promote themselves leading to frustration when managers take credit for their work. Additionally, they tend to neglect networking, making them vulnerable during layoffs of reorganizations since decision-makers don't know who they are.

Now, don't get me wrong- having a strong work ethic is commendable. However, it's crucial to refocus that energy on the right activities, and that's where the *Skyscraper Method* comes in. It will teach you how to pivot some of your efforts towards your passions while maintaining valuable connections. By striking the right balance between "head down" and "head up," you can build relationships with influential individuals and consistently make progress in your desired field or business area.

Keep in mind that achieving your ultimate goal – getting paid well for doing a job you enjoy– requires a long-term mindset. The *Skyscraper Method* isn't a quick fix or a one-time solution. It's a mentality and a process of continual career growth. The success you'll achieve by implementing the methods outlined in this book will come with time and consistency.

I'll be sharing more about my personal turning point career experience later, but in this chapter, let's break down the two key components that make up the *Skyscraper method*: Controlling your career trajectory and executing superior networking. The *Skyscraper Method* awaits, it's time to unlock your full potential!

Part 1. Control Career Trajectory

Over the past decade, I've had the pleasure of working with many mentees and clients, and one common frustration I've noticed among them is dissatisfaction with their careers. They often feel embarrassed about the series of jobs they've had up to this point. When I dig deeper into their frustrations, I'd often discover what I call a "career path gap." This occurs when the drawback of their current role outweighs the benefits and there's a clear disparity between their career experience and their career aspirations.

This gap can happen early on in one's career or even after several years of working in a company. Let me give you a couple of examples to illustrate this point:

Meet Tony, a client in his mid-twenties who recently landed a consultant role. After six months on the job, Tony realized that the actual responsibilities didn't align with what was promised during the interview process. Instead of the fast-paced environment and complex problem-solving he expected, he found himself doing data entry, client training, and back-end process improvement projects. Frustrated with his situation, Tony reached out to me for guidance. Together we identified the career path gap and devised an action plan to ensure he didn't end up in a similar situation in his next role.

Now let's talk about Kim, a seasoned manager at a marketing firm with 12 years of experience. During our introductory interview, Kim shared that the creative job she once enjoyed had turned into a stressful experience, thanks to a leadership reorganization. Her role had shifted from managing creative projects with extended timelines to overseeing technology and operations functions with tight deadlines. Her aspirations of becoming a Marketing Director managing creative projects were falling short of her actual experience. Kim, too, was living in a career path gap.

Both Tony and Kim found themselves growing increasingly frustrated with their current work situations, and they were losing sight of their next career moves. They had lost control of their career trajectories. Looking back on their career, they couldn't understand how they ended up where they were, and they had no idea where they were heading next.

To visualize your own career trajectory, think of it as an airplane's flight path. Imagine a pilot flying from Chicago to LA, setting the plane on autopilot, and then taking a nap. When the pilot wakes up 20 minutes later, they discover the plane is way off course above New York City. to make matters worse, they can't turn off autopilot! Can you imagine the fear, frustration, and confusion? The pilot is nowhere near their intended destination, unaware of where the plane is heading, and feels helpless to regain control.

Similarly, when you accept roles without a career plan, you're essentially putting your career on autopilot. If you keep accepting job after job without setting clear expectations, the career path gap will only widen. Eventually you'll wake up one day feeling frustrated and confused, just like our pilot. So, what's the solution? It's time to destroy the autopilot mode and take control of your career trajectory. How? Through three simple steps: reviewing your past career experiences, discovering what brought you joy in those experiences, and creating a plan to work in a profession that aligns with that enjoyment.

When working with clients who are experiencing a wide career path gap, our first step is to understand and document their career experiences. We delve into the challenges they face in their current career journeys. We ask questions like: Does their work fulfill them? What's their growth potential? What underutilized skills do they possess? Who do they network with and Why? The responses provide us with a clear picture of the direction their career path is heading.

Once clients have a grasp of their career journey, we move forward to uncover the passions that they have been ignited along that path. You might be wondering why finding passion is crucial. Well, in my view, discovering what you're genuinely passionate about is the starting point for finding enjoyment in your career. I take my clients (and you, shortly) through a series of thought-provoking questions and exercises to identify the activities in the workplace that make their hearts sing. We explore inquiries such as: What's something that makes you lose track of time when you're fully immersed in it? Additionally, we engage in exercises like creating a personal mission statement. These activities help reveal their professional passions.

As we progress, we align career goals with suitable occupations. For instance, if you find joy in reading and possess a keen attention to detail, pursuing a career as a professional editor might be an excellent fit. If you relish traveling and enjoy meeting new people, exploring opportunities as an international sales associate could be exciting for you. Alternatively, if you thrive on working with numbers independently, you might consider establishing your own statistical firm.

Through these exercises, I personally discovered my passions lie in helping others, creating new things, public speaking, and problem-solving. This realization led me to pursue roles that intersect with my passions as a career coach and project manager.

Once I found that intersection where my passions meet my professions, I devoted all my efforts to aligning my career goals with those passions. This final step is crucial to taking control of your career trajectory. It involves developing, aligning, and executing detailed goals to ensure that your career experience aligns with your career aspirations.

We achieve this by setting both short-term and long-term goals that directly correspond to your passionate profession. But it's not merely about jotting down these goals; it's about actively pursuing them and holding yourself accountable.

The execution process can feel overwhelming, so I strongly urge my clients to find an accountability partner who can serve as a soundboard, sergeant, and supporter. This allows for honest conversations about career goals and helps keep track progress toward achieving those goals.

In the forthcoming chapters, we will delve into exercises that will help you understand your career experiences, uncover your professional passion, and achieve passion-centered career goals. Once you have control of your career trajectory, you can take your career off autopilot and chart the course toward the destination you desire. Not only will you obtain a role that you genuinely enjoy, but you'll also envision where your career will be in the next 5-10 years.

Next, we will explore the second half of the *Skyscraper Method* equation: Execute Superior Networking.

Part 2. Execute Superior Networking

What is Networking?

In the upcoming chapters, I will provide you with a carefully crafted outline that will make networking effortless and empower you to develop exceptional relationship management skills capable of transforming your career. But before we dive into the fun, let's start with the basics.

According to the esteemed Merriam-Webster dictionary, networking is defined as "the exchange of information or services among individuals, groups, or institutions." However, I define networking in a simpler yet more profound way: it is the ability to strengthen weak connections with others. To me, networking is a powerful process of building relationships that holds the golden key to a thriving corporate career.

Think about it. How often do you encounter a high-level executive who doesn't possess an extensive list of influential contacts? These are the connections that lead organizations, foster business success, and create generational wealth. These executives have gained access to such valuable networks through the art of relationship building. And guess what? You can do the same!

How Do You Network?

Networking involves spending quality time with another business professional, engaging in discussions about personal and professional topics of interest.

In my experience, successful networking can be broken down into three stages: visibility, credibility, and trust. The concept is that visibility leads to credibility, which ultimately leads to trust.

Visibility represents the initial level of networking, where the people you meet become aware of who you are and what you do. Consistently showcasing your results establishes your credibility. When people recognize your competence based on their personal interactions, observed outcomes, or positive word-of-mouth, you gain credibility. Once you have established yourself as a credible individual, people will trust you and be more willing to share valuable information with you. Trust is the stage where the true magic of networking unfolds. It's when people know your abilities, understand your work, and are willing to refer you to others within their network. By applying the *Skyscraper Method* effectively, you can gain the trust of the right people who can elevate your career to new heights.

Who Should You Network with?

You might be wondering, who are the individuals you should aim to build trust with? I recommend seeking out leaders or peers who show a genuine interest in your success and can impact your career through their words or actions. From this point forward, I'll refer to these professionals as your influencers.

As you expand your network, it's important to identify influencers who possess certain attributes. They should have a wealth of knowledge about your industry, a broad network, or a perspective that you admire.

Networking with an influencer who possesses a wealth of knowledge can provide invaluable insights into your future options within your industry. It's like having a glimpse into a crystal ball. These mentors are willing to share their vast experiences with you and answer important questions such as: What skills do I need to acquire to increase my earning potential? What steps can I take today to reach the executive level? Am I investing my time wisely in my current role? How can I effectively manage my manager? If your influencer is an executive with numerous direct reports, they not only offer job opportunities but also provide a deep understanding of how executives think and operate.

Additionally, networking with an influencer who may not have direct reports but has a vast network of connections can be highly beneficial. These professionals often serve on various committees and bring wisdom, experience, and valuable contacts to the table. Networking with this type of influencer can be particularly rewarding because they usually enjoy mentoring others. Once you have gained their trust, they will gladly introduce you to anyone within their sphere of influence. This becomes especially advantageous if you are considering a career switch, as they can craft warm email introductions to key contacts in your desired industry.

Lastly, it is valuable to network with an influencer who possesses a perspective that you admire. I personally enjoy meeting with influencers who challenge my thinking and offer suggestions to enhance my skills. Within the framework of the

Skyscraper Method, you can engage in healthy debates and support each other in achieving your respective goals.

Who should you avoid networking with?

This question may seem straightforward, but not every person you encounter is the right fit for networking. To effectively implement the *Skyscraper Method*, you must approach networking with purpose and intent. Most of your networking discussions will be engaging and fruitful, adding value to your career plans. However, there will be instances where the conversations fall short. These are the discussions you should steer clear of. Typically, these devaluing conversations occur due to the intentions of the influencer. Look out for signs such as ignoring emails, evading questions, or monopolizing the conversation by only talking about themselves. While these instances are rare, when they do happen, my advice is to gracefully end that networking relationship.

Cutting off a leader from your network is not an easy decision, but in certain cases, it becomes necessary. I once connected with a senior risk manager from a company of interest. My goal was to learn about him, his organization, and potential job opportunities. However, during our initial interaction, when I inquired about details regarding his company, I received vague and indirect responses filled with fluff. I gave it one more chance, only to receive the same result. At that point, I made the decision not to proceed with the professional relationship and expressed that I would reconnect when our priorities aligned once again.

Why would someone want to network with you?

Well, there are several compelling reasons that can make you an attractive networking partner. First and foremost, you bring a unique perspective and a fresh point of view to the table, especially when it comes to hot topics and current issues. Let's take the recent focus on social injustice as an example. During networking sessions, I've had the pleasure of learning from a mentee about the viral nature of donation requests for social responsibility organizations on social media. Your ability to offer insightful perspectives like these makes you a valuable connection in the networking realm.

Furthermore, your personal story holds great appeal. It encompasses the hurdles you've overcome in the past, the challenges you face in the present, and the endless possibilities that lie ahead. When the opportunity arises, don't hesitate to share your story with your network. By showing vulnerability and engaging in storytelling, you forge deeper connections with your mentors and colleagues.

Lastly, let's not forget about the power of your own network. Just as influencers can share their professional connections to support your career goals, you possess your own network filled with valuable contacts and connections. When the occasion presents itself, be open to reciprocating by sharing these personal connections. Over the years, my mentees have connected me with invaluable professional services like family photographers, nanny services, and even a personal chef. This exchange of resources and support strengthens the bond between networking partners.

Always remember that networking is a two-way street. It should be mutually beneficial, with both parties deriving value from the conversation and relationship. If the value is absent or the connection isn't aligning with your goals, it's perfectly acceptable to politely conclude that networking relationship. In the upcoming chapters, we will dive into the tactical aspects of networking, exploring when to network and what to say during networking interactions. Get ready to refine your networking skills and make meaningful connections that will propel your career forward.

Myths about Networking

I want to debunk some common myths about networking that might be holding you back. It's time to set the record straight and show you how networking can be a game-changer in your career. So, let's dive in and demystify these statements, one by one.

1. *"I need to be an extrovert to be good at networking."*
FALSE. Let me tell you, networking prowess is not limited to extroverts. Your personality traits don't define your networking skills. Sure, it might feel uncomfortable at first, but with practice, preparation, and a willingness to put yourself out there, your discomfort will diminish over time. It's all about honing your networking abilities through repetition and embracing the process.

2. *"Networking is only for networking events."*
FALSE. Networking events can be overwhelming and not always the best place to make meaningful connections. The real networking magic happens in unexpected places, like your workplace. Every interaction, whether in the parking lot, elevator, meeting, or cafeteria, holds the potential to forge valuable

connections that can elevate your career. Keep your eyes open and seize these daily networking opportunities.

Now, here's a hidden gem for you. I've found seminars and conferences to be a gold mine for networking. After listening to an inspiring executive keynote speaker, take advantage of the smaller setting and connect with them. Summon your courage, approach the speaker during the post-event networking session, and strike up a conversation. This small step can lead to invaluable relationships with leaders in your field of interest. Remember, taking risks is how you make big leaps in your career.

3. *"I don't need to maintain my contacts; they will always be there for me."*
FALSE. Your professional relationships are like plants. If you neglect them, they wither away. That coffee talk you had with an executive three years ago won't hold much weight if you haven't kept in touch. Executives have busy lives, and if you don't nurture the connection over time, they might forget who you are. Sustained communication is key to maintaining and benefiting from your network.

4. *"I don't have time to network because my job is too demanding."*
FALSE. Let's get one thing straight: you have time for what truly matters. Networking is an investment in your future that can yield life-changing results. Imaging someone offering you a dream home or a shiny new sports car in exchange for just a 30-minute conversation. You'd find the time, no questions asked. So, the real issue here is your motivation and the why behind your career aspirations. Once you have the right

motivation, committing to the time investment becomes a no-brainer. Remember, networking can unlock opportunities that lead to your wildest dreams.

5. *"It's hard to meet people at my job."*
MAYBE. Look, your workplace might not be the easiest place to naturally make connections, but trust me, networking is possible anywhere. It's all about your approach. By applying the tactics outlined in this book, you'll develop the skills to connect with others effortlessly. Networking will become second nature, and you'll be amazed at the opportunities that come your way.

6. *"Networking is a waste of time."*
MAYBE. Networking can indeed be a waste of time if you approach it without purpose and genuine engagement. Meaningless conversations won't get you anywhere. But fear not, my friend. You've got this book in your hands, and it will equip you with the knowledge to have fruitful networking conversations that lead to real results. Say goodbye to the wasted time and hello to meaningful connections.

7. *"Networking is scary."*
TRUE. Let's face it, networking can be scary, even for me. As a kid, I was terrified of meeting new people at summer camp. But once I got to know them, I realized what amazing connections I had made. The same goes for us as adults. To overcome that initial fear, preparation is key. Practice networking, never stop networking, and watch your confidence grow. Soon enough, you'll find yourself excited for networking opportunities, ready to seize them with enthusiasm.

8. *"There is no value in networking."*
FALSE. This, my friends, is the biggest myth of all. Networking holds unlimited value. I'll go as far as saying it's just as important as your day-to-day job. Building a strong network has been a game-changer in my own career. Having a network that will go to bat for you, vouch for you, and create opportunities for you is an incredible feeling. Without networking, you might find yourself working twice as hard to achieve your goals. So, let go of this myth, embrace the power of networking, and watch your career soar to new heights.

Remember, networking is the key to unlocking a world of possibilities. It's time to dispel these myths, embrace the art of connecting, and witness the transformative impact it can have on your career.

Difference between Networking and Superior Networking

If you're reading this, I can already tell you're hungry for success and ready to unlock your full potential. Well, strap in because I'm about to introduce you to a game-changer: superior networking. Now, you might be thinking, "Timothy, what's so special about superior networking?" Buckle up, because I'm about to show you how to take your networking skills to a whole new level.

Superior networking isn't about collecting business cards like a desperate socialite or attending tedious events that drain your energy. Oh no, we're flipping the script here. It's time to approach networking like a savvy entrepreneur on a mission.

We're talking about strategic connections, meaningful relationships, and a damn good time while we're at it.

Forget about the old adage of "it's not what you know, it's who you know." In the world of superior networking, it's about who knows you and what you bring to the table. We're going to focus on creating a buzz around your name, positioning yourself as the go-to-person in your industry or field. We're not talking about cultivating a network of power players who not only know your name but are eager to support your rise to the top.

Now, I want you to imagine a network filled with high-level influencers, industry mavens, and game-changers who are ready to open doors for you. Picture yourself walking into a room with confidence, knowing that you've strategically connected with the right people. With superior networking, you're able to tap into a goldmine of opportunities, collaborations, and mentorship that can catapult your career to unprecedented heights.

Benefits of Superior Networking

(1) Gain a personal career coach
When you network effectively, you create a safe space of influencers and industry leaders to coach you through any career concerns you may have. Through superior networking, you can have a solid soundboard, a trusted confidant, with whom you can be vulnerable about your career and take decisive action. It's all about having those honest conversations that propel you forward.

(2) Develop long-lasting relationships with a leader
Over time, relationships built from superior networking can go beyond the corporate domain and create genuine personal connections. It's about letting your guard down and being open to mixing work and personal relationships with executive leaders. These connections become more than just business interactions; they become pillars of support and guidance in your journey.

(3) Find your dream career
When you engage in authentic, vulnerable conversations about your career passions within your network, you'll be amazed at the opportunities that can come your way. Your network becomes a catalyst, connecting you to job openings and prospects aligned with your true passions. It's like unlocking a hidden realm of possibilities.

(4) Gain job security
With a strong network, an influential leader might give you a heads-up about potential career pitfalls like corporate reorganization. They become your inside source, willing to help you navigate these challenges. This benefit is priceless, especially if you value career stability. I experienced it firsthand when my company went through a major reorg. Thanks to a mentor within my network who broke confidentiality to warn me, I had time to secure a new career opportunity before my team was dissolved. That's the power of superior networking, my friends.

But here's the kicker: superior networking isn't just about what you can get from others; it's about what you can give. We're talking about adding massive value to every interaction, becoming a sought-after resource, and making it rain opportunities from others. By becoming a connector, a trusted advisor, and a go-giver, you'll build a network that's not only powerful but also deeply meaningful and fulfilling.

In closing, networking is a powerful tool that can propel your career to new heights. By strategically building relationships with influencers who can provide knowledge, connections, and unique perspectives, you open doors to opportunities and growth. Remember to approach networking with an open mind, be genuine in your interactions, and always seek to add value to others. As you apply the principles of visibility, credibility, and trust, coupled with the *Skyscraper Method*, you'll discover that networking becomes not just a professional endeavor, but a fulfilling journey of personal and professional development. Embrace the power of networking and watch as it transforms your career trajectory and opens up a world of possibilities.

The *Skyscraper Method* Phases:

Just like the timeless skyscrapers that grace the New York City skyline, constructing a successful career requires careful planning, a solid foundation, a great team, and effective execution. The *Skyscraper Method*, inspired by these magnificent structures, follows a series of phases that mirror the development process. Let's dive into the eight phases:

- Phase 1: Assessing your past career experiences
- Phase 2: Digging to discover your current career desires

- Phase 3: Framing out your future career aspirations
- Phase 4: Structuring an Foundational networking plan
- Phase 5: Building a network of Leaders
- Phase 6: Strengthening connections through servicing
- Phase 7: Finalizing supportive methods
- Phase 8: Opening your Career Skyscraper

In each phase, I'll provide you with valuable tips, tools, and assignments to inspire and motivate you in building a career that reaches great heights.

Now, let's focus on the first phase of the *Skyscraper Method*, where we assess your career experiences to answer a crucial question: How did you get "here"? Through thought-provoking questions and a career health check, we'll uncover any gaps in your career path and gain a deeper understanding of its unique characteristics. This initial step sets the foundation for making informed decisions to steer your career trajectory in the right direction.

▶ Phase 1: Assessing

Skyscraper Method

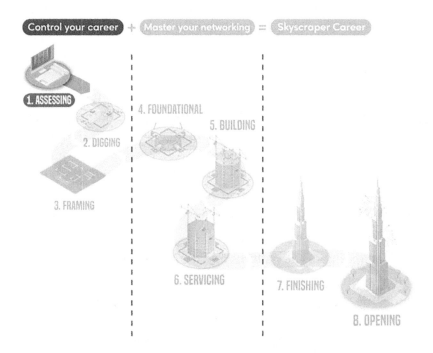

Imagine you've stumbled upon a prime piece of real estate in the heart of a bustling city. It's like winning the lottery! You're itching to develop something truly remarkable, a building that will be the talk of the town. But, oh no, there's already a structure standing there. What's a developer to do? Demolish and start from scratch or work with what's already there?

Now, let me tell you, just like in building development, when it comes to your career, you need a solid plan. Metaphorically, the land represents your career growth potential, and the existing structure symbolizes the career you've built up until now. To recreate your dream career, we've got to assess the past, figure out how we got "here."

Assessing past career experiences is the first phase of the *Skyscraper Method*. It's like conducting a thorough inspection before you start knocking down walls. We'll start by asking some key questions, a career health check if you will, to identify areas for improvement and growth. It's like doing a check-up on your career's well-being. And hey, while we're at it, we'll also review and update your professional footprint—your resume, LinkedIn profile, and all that jazz.

By evaluating your professional footprint, you'll gain a bird's-eye view of your career history. Think of it as stepping back and surveying the landscape before you start building that dream skyscraper. This will not only give you a clearer understanding of the patterns and trends in your career journey but also prepare you for new job opportunities that may come knocking.

Once we've completed the Assessment phase, you'll have the tools and insights you need to start the career reconstruction process. It's time to put on that hard hat and get to work on building the career of your dreams. Together, we'll design a blueprint that aligns with your passions, skills, and goals, and create a career that stands tall, strong, and unforgettable.

So, my fellow career architects, get ready to assess, revamp, and construct the career path that will make others look up in awe. It's time to create a professional masterpiece that will leave a lasting legacy!

Chapter 2:
Career Health Check

Let's talk about this career health check. It's like giving your career a full-body exam, but without the awkward hospital gown. We'll go through a series of questions that will dig deep into various aspects of your professional life. And don't worry, there won't be any pop quizzes or math equations involved!

The purpose of this career health check is to give you a panoramic view of your career situation. It's all about gaining clarity and insight into your current circumstances. We'll evaluate your level of satisfaction, identify any gaps or misalignments, and pinpoint areas that need a little extra love and attention.

Now, let's get down to business. These questions cover everything from your goals and values to your skills and interests. We'll dive deep into your personal fulfillment, work-life balance, growth opportunities, and job satisfaction. Oh, and we can't forget about the importance of networking. Building connections is like having a secret weapon in your career arsenal.

As we go through these questions, my goal is to provide you with personalized guidance and support. I want you to walk away with a clear understanding of where you stand in terms of your career health. Think of it as a roadmap to success, a blueprint to help you navigate the twists and turns of your professional journey.

So, let's buckle up and dive into this career health check. Together, we'll uncover whether you're in control of your career path, if you're building the right connections, and which direction your career is currently heading. Consider it a fun and enlightening adventure, with yours truly as your trusty guide through the maze of career possibilities.

Are you in control of your career path?

Understanding if you're in control of your career path is absolutely crucial. It's about taking charge and owning your professional journey. When you recognize that you have the power to shape your own destiny, it fuels your drive to seek out opportunities, set meaningful goals, and make intentional choices that align with your dreams. This sense of control instills a proactive mindset and fuels your hunger for continuous learning and growth.

Importantly, knowing your level of control equips you to navigate obstacles and setbacks with resilience. Embracing the fact that you have the power to adapt and make choices empowers you to bounce back from failures, learn valuable lessons, and adjust your strategies when faced with roadblocks. This mindset not only enables you to thrive in the face of adversity but also opens unexpected doors and paves the way for remarkable opportunities.

In a nutshell, understanding whether you're in control of your career path is crucial. It's about taking ownership, making informed decisions, and actively shaping your trajectory. Recognizing your level of control empowers you to gain clarity, pursue meaningful goals, invest in your skill set, and navigate challenges with resilience. Ultimately, this self-awareness allows you to create a career that aligns with your vision and leads to long-term success and fulfillment.

CAREER HEALTH CHECK 1/5

Are you in control of your career path?

Let's dive into assessing your control over your career path with a few key questions:

1. Do you have a clear vision of where you want to be in your career in the next three years?

2. Do you set specific goals and milestones to guide your career progression?

3. Are you comfortable with taking calculated risks and exploring new career paths?

4. Does the work you do at your job feel meaningful and fulfilling?

5. Do you have decision-making power in shaping your work and projects?

6. Do you discuss your current or future career expectations with colleagues?

7. Do your career moves align with your purpose?

These questions are designed to help gauge your level of self-direction, proactiveness, goal setting, adaptability, and overall control in shaping your career path. Evaluating these aspects can help identify areas where you may need support or guidance to take greater control of your professional trajectory.

Are you building the right connections?

Knowing how to build the right professional connections is an absolute game-changer for employees. Let me tell you why. Building meaningful connections in your industry isn't just about collecting business cards or attending events for the sake of it. It's about cultivating relationships that can unlock doors, create opportunities, and propel your career forward at warp speed.

Why is it so important? Well, the right connections can provide you with invaluable knowledge and insights that can't be found in any textbook. By surrounding yourself with experts and experienced professionals, you gain access to a wealth of wisdom, guidance, and real-world advice. These connections can help you navigate the intricacies of your industry, offer insider tips, and share valuable lessons learned from their own journeys. In short, they become your secret weapon in the pursuit of professional success.

In the end, knowing how to build the right professional connections is a superpower that can accelerate your career growth. By surrounding yourself with knowledgeable individuals, you gain access to valuable insights and guidance. Additionally, these connections can open doors to exciting opportunities and become your advocates in the industry. So, let's find out how you've been doing with your professional relationships.

CAREER HEALTH CHECK 2/5

Are you building the right connections?

Let's evaluate your networking prowess with a few important questions:

1. Do you actively engage in building connections beyond the initial encounter?

2. Are you known for being a resourceful and helpful person within your professional circles?

3. Do you maintain and nurture existing connections by staying in touch?

4. If you were suddenly without a job today, could you rely on your connections to help you find another opportunity? Is your network robust and supportive in times of need?

5. Do you regularly meet with leaders from different organizations, approaching these meetings with clear goals and objectives? Are you proactive in seeking connections with influential individuals?

6. Do you engage in one-on-one conversations with new contacts to build deeper connections and learn from their experiences?

7. Do you often learn about job openings before they are posted online? Are you well-connected and informed within your industry?

These questions aim to assess your networking efforts and your ability to establish meaningful connections. They focus on your willingness to engage with others, provide support, and maintain professional relationships. Evaluating

CAREER HEALTH CHECK 2/5 *(cont)*

these aspects can help you determine if you are effectively leveraging networking opportunities to build a valuable professional network.

If you answered "No" to any of these questions, don't worry. There is room for growth and improvement. I'll provide you with details, tips, tricks, and actionable steps to enhance your networking skills. Together, we'll work towards developing into a superior networker, expanding your professional connections, and opening new doors of opportunity.

Career in Action Activity: Self Reflection 101

Go back through the questions and document the responses where you answered "No." These are your career opportunities, areas where you can focus on making improvements and taking charge. Throughout this book, we'll keep track of these responses to help you navigate and make progress on your career journey.

Now that we've assessed the health of your career trajectory and the strength of your professional network, it's time to tackle the final section of the Career Health Check: determining which direction your career is currently heading. Brace yourself, because we're about to face some career storms.

What are these career storms, you ask? Well, they're unexpected changes that can shake the foundations of your professional journey. They can come in the form of layoffs, industry shifts, or even personal circumstances that force you to reconsider your path. But fear not, because we're going to evaluate how prepared you are to weather these storms and come out stronger on the other side.

Chapter 3:
A Storm is Coming

In the unpredictable world of corporate America, we're bound to encounter some unavoidable and unfortunate situations. Picture it like facing a powerful storm—company reorganizations, mass layoffs, sudden changes in job responsibilities. These events, I like to call career storms. They hit us without warning, and no matter how hard we try, we can't stop them from happening.

Think about the last hurricane you experienced. You knew it was coming, and there was no way to prevent it. But what did you do? You prepared accordingly, seeking shelter in a place that was strong enough to protect you and your loved ones. You wouldn't choose to weather a Category 3 hurricane in a flimsy tent, right? That wouldn't be smart or safe.

Well, just like rainstorms, career storms can shake us to the core. They force us to search for new job opportunities and rebuild our careers. These storms can take many forms—negative feedback, a tyrant boss, company reorganizations, or even job termination.

Negative feedback from colleagues, bosses, or executives can cause anxiety and make us question our place in the professional world. A ruthless boss can create a toxic and stressful work environment that takes a toll on our well-being. Company reorganizations can shuffle the hierarchy, altering roles, responsibilities, teams, and leadership, instantly turning a job we once loved into one we despise. And job termination, well, that can be demoralizing, humiliating, and make us feel like we're starting from scratch.

Depending on our level of preparation, any of these career storms can hinder, slow down, or completely halt our career growth and development in our current role.

If you've experienced one of these storms, you probably found yourself contemplating or forced to make a career change. Career storms push us to reassess, adjust, and make decisions about our professional paths. However, what truly matters is not the storm itself, but how we survive it. That's what this chapter is all about—helping you think about the type of career you need to create in order to weather these storms and emerge stronger on the other side.

So, buckle up and prepare yourself, because we're about to navigate the treacherous seas of career storms together. Let's equip you with the tools and mindset to not just survive but thrive in the face of adversity. It's time to build a career that can withstand any storm that comes your way.

The Career Classifications

As a seasoned career coach, it's evident that those who are living the career they envisioned are the ones in control of their career journey. They not only find joy in their work but also have a sense of fulfillment. On the other hand, those who are not experiencing the career they had envisioned are lacking control over their career journey. They either tolerate the work they do, going through the motions without enthusiasm, or completely dislike their job. So, let's determine where you stand on this spectrum by reflecting on your current career satisfaction. Ask yourself, do you tolerate or truly enjoy the work you do?

During our initial conversation, if I notice that discussing your work triggers anxiety, leads to a laundry list of complaints, or leaves you emotionally detached, it's a clear indication that you simply tolerate your career. On the flip side, if you are intentional about your career moves, energized by the impact you make as part of a team, and passionate about specific aspects of your work, it's safe to say that you genuinely enjoy what you do. To be honest, that's the ultimate goal for all my clients—I want them to radiate pure delight whenever the topic of work arises.

Now, let's shift gears and talk about networking. In my experience, there are two tiers: superior networking and inferior networking. It's a binary distinction—either you network with a clear purpose or you don't. There's really no middle ground here. Superior networkers are those individuals who excel at networking. They actively build valuable relationships with peers, mentors, or mentees, recognizing the power of these connections. On the other hand, inferior networkers engage in networking without a true purpose, meeting with other professionals sporadically or not at all. So, which type of networker are you? Are you superior or inferior in your networking efforts?

Drawing from my interactions with thousands of corporate professionals and discussions about their career paths, I've identified four distinct career classifications that individuals tend to fall into. These classifications reflect the career paths they have built based on their level of networking (Superior/Inferior) and career satisfaction (Tolerate/Enjoy). It's important to note that everyone working in corporate America can be grouped into one of these four classifications.

As we explore each classification, I'll be using building structures as metaphors to represent them. This will help you visualize and relate to the characteristics of each classification. I want you to reflect on your own professional journey and assess which classification aligns with your current career path. Regardless of your current classification, the purpose of this assessment is to uncover areas of opportunity that can lead to career fulfillment and the development of a powerful network. You'll find a visual summary of each classification in the chart below.

Join me, as I use illustrative stories to describe each of the four career classifications.

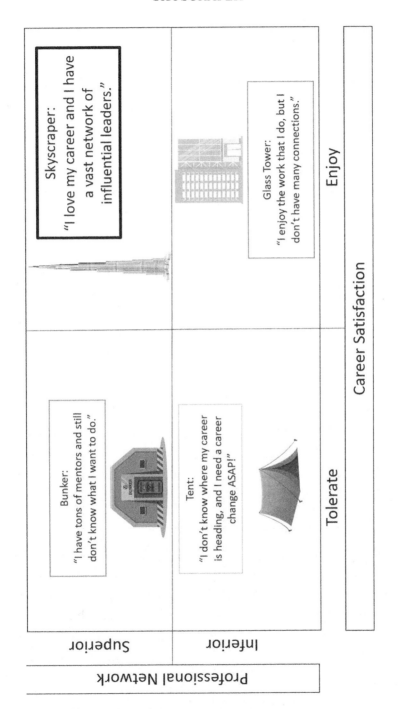

The Tent

Let's talk about the most prevalent career classification—one that many people unknowingly find themselves in. I call it the "tent" career classification. Imagine a professional who envisions a more fulfilling and successful career, but hasn't taken any significant steps to make that vision a reality. They find themselves stuck in a job they don't really like, but they stay because of the comfort of a regular paycheck. Moreover, they lack the urgency to network and explore other opportunities.

Now, think of a physical tent used for camping outdoors. It provides shelter and protection from the elements and critters that roam around at night. However, a tent wouldn't hold up well in severe weather conditions. Similarly, the career journey of someone in the tent career classification would crumble under the weight of a career storm due to their lack of networking efforts and confidence in their chosen career path.

Let me introduce you to Levon (not his real name), a client who found himself trapped in the midst of a career storm. Levon had always dreamt of achieving great things in the field of sales. Unfortunately, his lack of networking efforts and fluctuating self-belief proved to be his downfall.

As his company underwent a major restructuring, Levon's role took a hit. To make matters worse, he had a difficult manager who showed little support for his projects and favored other teams with lucrative deals. While his colleagues, who had built strong networks and established themselves as valuable assets, smoothly transitioned into new positions, Levon felt lost and uncertain about his future. The absence of connections and dwindling confidence made it challenging for him to explore alternative opportunities or seek guidance from mentors.

As time passed, Levon witnessed his colleagues thrive while he struggled to regain his footing. Without a robust network, he remained oblivious to potential job openings and industry trends. His lack of confidence further hindered his ability to take proactive steps towards his career goals. He began doubting his abilities and questioning whether his chosen career path was right for him. He felt overwhelmed and stuck in a state of inertia—until he reached out to me.

When I encounter clients in such situations, my aim is to help them strategically transition out of that role. Together, we create a career action plan that guides them towards discovering their true professional passion. This way, their next career move not only contributes to their personal growth but also aligns with their deepest aspirations. Without clarity on career direction or a strong network, professionals in the tent classification often find themselves switching jobs that don't propel their growth or, worse, remaining trapped in an unhealthy environment.

The tent career classification is built by individuals who yearn for upward mobility but fail to take the necessary steps for meaningful career changes. If this resonates with you and you're eager for more from your professional journey, perhaps it's time for a change. Let me share an example of someone with a tent classification career that has left a lasting impression on me.

Tent Man: Where I do NOT want to be in 20 years?

Twenty years ago, I was a young, energetic analyst at a Wall Street firm in the heart of Lower Manhattan. It was my first taste of corporate America and my initial step into the working world after college. During my early days at the firm, I quickly earned two nicknames: "the kick ass analyst" for my efficient quantitative skills and modeling abilities, and "the Corporate Bookie" for organizing friendly football bets among my coworkers. As the bookie, I didn't participate in the bets myself but ensured fair play by distributing the winnings to the lucky victors. This role allowed me to meet colleagues from across the company, discussing everything from bets and football to office politics and hot topics of the day. Little did I know that a random encounter would shape my perspective on work forever.

One day, as I engaged in a lively conversation with a colleague about the championship hopes of my beloved New York Jets, I was interrupted by an older gentleman. His raspy voice caught me off guard, as I hadn't even noticed him in his cubicle until he spoke up. "How old are you, son?" he asked, abruptly cutting me off. I responded with a smile, "I'm 25, sir." The older gentleman, sporting thick black glasses, a smurf blue fleece sweater, and oversized khaki pants, returned my smile, resembling a department store Santa. Then he uttered words that would leave a lasting impact on me: "You're just a baby. When you were five, I started working here," he said, tapping his desk with his index finger.

I was taken aback. Surely, he couldn't mean that he had been sitting in the same spot for the past 20 years. I scratched my head and asked, "Oh, so you've been with the company since the '80s?" He replied with a mix of pain and resignation in his voice, "Yes! It's been a painful ride, but this has been my cube ever since - my very own cube." His words shook me to the core, as if his job had become a burden he carried through life. At that moment, I made a silent promise to myself: I would not let my career become a stagnant burden like his.

Reflecting on the encounter, I realized that by not closing the gap in his career path, he had become trapped in a job that didn't fulfill him. His career had become a metaphorical tent. It was a wake-up call for me, igniting a fire within. From that point on, I started pondering my long-term goals and crafting a plan for my future career. Meeting that man became the catalyst for my *skyscraper method*, even though I wasn't aware of it at the time. He inspired me to dream and contemplate what I truly desired for my future. Luckily, I had the luxury of time to figure it out, being only an entry-level professional when our paths crossed.

That encounter shaped my career aspirations. I vowed to maximize my natural talents, seek out a job that truly brought me joy, and constantly strive for growth. I moved on from that role, actively networking, pursuing advanced degrees, and gaining valuable experiences along the way. Throughout the years, I often wondered about the fate of the "tent man" and whether he ever found happiness. He became a constant reminder of who I did not want to become. And if you've picked up this book, chances are you share that sentiment too. So, keep reading, because together we'll ensure that you don't find yourself stuck in a career path like his.

CAREER HEALTH CHECK 3/5

Are you building a Tent?

Here are a few questions I use to help employees realize if they are in a dead-end job and need to find a career that brings them satisfaction and the opportunity to build a stronger network. Take a moment and reflect on these questions.

1. Are you yawning your way through the workday, feeling unchallenged and as stagnant as a puddle on a rainy day?

2. Do you feel like a hidden gem, with your contributions going unnoticed and unappreciated?

3. Are you daydreaming of a career that's a perfect match for your passions, values, and long-term goals?

4. Are you yearning to break free from the shackles of mediocrity and unleash your full potential?

5. Are you currently experiencing a lack of growth and advancement opportunities in your current position?

6. Have you noticed a lack of recognition or appreciation for your contributions in your current job?

7. Do you find it difficult to build meaningful connections and expand your professional network within your industry?

These questions are designed to prompt you to reflect on your current job situation and evaluate whether you are in a dead-end job that offers little satisfaction and limited networking opportunities.

If the answer to these questions is a resounding "Yes!" Then it's time to take action and make that move towards a

CAREER HEALTH CHECK 3/5 *(cont)*

job you genuinely enjoy. But don't worry, I won't leave you hanging. I want you to focus on all the phases within the skyscraper method. This method will serve you by guiding you through the steps necessary to transition from that dead-end situation to a fulfilling career that brings you both satisfaction and the chance to build a robust professional network. Together, we'll uncover your true passions, set meaningful goals, and take strategic actions to propel you towards a career that lights you up. It's time to break free from the chains of that dead-end job and embrace the possibilities that lie ahead.

The Bunker

Let's explore the intriguing world of the bunker career classification. This grouping is for professionals who find themselves in roles they don't enjoy and are stuck in a state of career stagnation. But here's the twist—those within the bunker classification are masters of networking. Think of them as social butterflies fluttering around the water cooler, engaging in informational interviews with top executives, and building an extensive web of professional relationships.

Now, imagine a bunker nestled deep in the woods. It provides shelter and protection from natural disasters like tornadoes, forest fires, or even Category 5 hurricanes. Similarly, professionals with a bunker career seamlessly navigate between jobs, avoiding the chaos of career storms. They rely on their networking prowess to unlock alternate job opportunities.

However, like the low height of a bunker, these individuals often miss out on career advancement and promotions. They need a reprioritization to discover their professional passion and pursue their dream job.

How do we identify a bunker classification? Well, there are two telltale signs. Firstly, when discussing career goals, these professionals struggle to articulate their future plans because they're unsure of what truly brings them joy. They might say something like, "I have countless mentors, but I'm not sure what I want to do." Secondly, a pattern of short-term jobs or job hopping emerges. Bunkers tend to switch roles frequently, often within the same year. While this allows them to leverage their connections, it also comes with the risk of burning bridges.

Now, let me share a captivating short story of a recent encounter with a bunker. Brace yourself for an enlightening tale that will shed light on the unique challenges and opportunities faced by individuals trapped in a bunker classification.

The Networking Enthusiast

Meet Alix (not her real name), a professional who possessed an extraordinary talent for networking. Alix was a force to be reckoned with, attending industry events, conferences, and social gatherings with unwavering enthusiasm, always seeking to expand her network and forge new connections.

At first, Alix's networking prowess seemed like a superpower. She amassed a vast circle of professional acquaintances, collecting business cards and LinkedIn connections like trophies.

Alix exuded confidence, navigating any professional situation with ease. However, as time went on, she encountered a significant challenge.

The first hurdle Alix faced was her struggle to maintain a job due to her overwhelming focus on networking. She would spend countless hours engaged in small talk, attending numerous meetups, and socializing with colleagues. Unfortunately, this came at the expense of neglecting her core responsibilities and meeting job expectations. Consequently, she found herself unable to hold onto a job for an extended period.

Alix's excessive networking not only impacted her work performance but also tarnished her professional reputation. Opportunities for growth and advancement eluded her due to her reputation as a "networking enthusiast" overshadowing her actual skills and accomplishments.

Realizing the negative consequences of her networking obsession, Alix sought my guidance and support. We discussed the importance of striking a balance between networking and fulfilling professional responsibilities. Alix made a conscious effort to prioritize her work, ensuring that she met the expectations of her job while still fostering meaningful connections.

With this newfound approach, Alix began to regain stability in her career. By focusing on delivering exceptional work, she rebuilt her professional reputation and earned the respect of her peers and superiors. Simultaneously, she continued to leverage her networking skills to advance her career, but this time with a more strategic and balanced approach.

Alix's journey taught her the crucial lesson of finding harmony between networking and maintaining a steady job. By prioritizing her work and delivering results, she demonstrated her commitment and dedication to her employers, thus allowing her networking efforts to enhance her career rather than hinder it.

Consequently, Alix's story serves as a valuable reminder that excessive networking, without a strong foundation of professional achievements, can hinder rather than enhance one's career. Striking the right balance between networking and maintaining a strong work ethic is key to long-term success.

CAREER HEALTH CHECK 4/5

Have you built a Bunker?

Are you one of those professionals who excel at networking but struggle to invest in career growth and find a fulfilling role? These questions will help you evaluate if your socializing habits are impacting your productivity and performance at work. Consider them to determine if your career path resembles that of a Bunker:

1. Do you find yourself often engaged in casual conversations with coworkers during work hours?

2. Do you find it challenging to stay focused on your tasks due to engaging in social conversations or activities with coworkers?

3. Are you frequently initiating or participating in non-work-related conversations during team meetings or work-related discussions?

CAREER HEALTH CHECK 4/5 *(cont)*

4. Have you received any feedback or comments from your supervisor or colleagues regarding excessive socializing in the workplace?

5. Do you often find yourself participating in social activities during work hours, such as organizing or attending social events or gatherings?

6. Are you frequently using personal electronic devices or social media for socializing purposes during work hours?

7. Has your productivity or work performance been negatively affected due to excessive socializing in the workplace?

If you answered "Yes" to any of these then you might find yourself fitting into the bunker career classification, don't worry! The tools in the upcoming sections of this book will be your secret weapons to recalibrate your career path. They will help you break free from the unhappiness of your current job and propel you towards a future where you truly enjoy your work and experience remarkable career growth. And here's the best part: you already have an established network at your disposal, which can become the key to unlocking unimaginable heights in your career.

The Glass Tower

"King Kong ain't got Sh*t on me!"

In the critically acclaimed film *Training Day*, Denzel Washington's character, Alonzo, utters that powerful line. It's a moment of desperation for Alonzo, a corrupt cop whose world comes crashing down when his criminal activities are exposed. He realizes he's alone, standing tall in a crowd that offers no support. Alonzo's character represents the "glass tower" in the community—a symbol of success and achievement without the meaningful connections that matter. But when faced with adversity, that glass tower crumbles.

In the world of corporate America, the Glass Tower career classification mirrors this delicate foundation. It signifies professionals who have climbed the ladder of success but lack the crucial networking skills to build meaningful connections. Whether you're a mid-level manager, a director, or an executive, the absence of a strong network leaves you vulnerable and isolated when a career storm strikes.

If you find yourself in this career classification, I want to congratulate you on discovering your professional passion. It's fantastic to meet someone who truly enjoys their work. I understand that networking can be daunting, but don't worry. In the upcoming chapters, I'll provide you with actionable steps to improve your network and transform your glass tower into a towering skyscraper.

Don't waste your potential!

Let me tell you a story about a remarkable individual, code name Bailee Ball. After completing business school, Bailee joined a rotational development program as a Product Manager. Among our team of talented professionals, Bailee stood out like a shining star. With her vibrant hair and introverted energy, she possessed an unmatched ability to single-handedly complete projects that would typically require an entire team. Her passion for creating new products and her exceptional quantitative skills made her the superstar on our team. Management recognized her talents and she received multiple promotions, cementing her reputation as a rockstar in our organization.

However, our team's journey took an unexpected and unfortunate turn when leadership made the decision to disband us. It was a sudden and jarring change that brought all ongoing projects to an abrupt halt for Bailee and the rest of the new product team. We found ourselves in a state of uncertainty, scrambling to find new job opportunities. I was fortunate to have the protection of my rotational program, but for Bailee, despite her exceptional track record, she faced a challenging road ahead. Her talents and achievements were largely unknown outside of our leadership team, making it difficult for her to secure a new position within the company.

Fast forward a few years, I crossed paths with Bailee at a local brewery. I discovered that she had indeed found a job after the layoff, but it was in sales. As a sales manager, Bailee was unhappy with the competitive nature of the role and frustrated by the office politics. She desperately desired a career change.

I could relate to her situation and offered a suggestion that aligned with her skillset. I recommended that she reconnect with our old teammates and explore opportunities in product management once again. However, Bailee revealed that networking and maintaining professional connections were her weaknesses. Her "I can do it myself" attitude, which had made her an exceptional product manager, now hindered her from reaching out for assistance. Bailee's glass tower career path had been struck by a brick, leaving her in a position similar to

Alonzo from Training Day—successful in her career, yet lacking a support network and silently yearning for help.

Bailee's story serves as a powerful reminder of the importance of networking and building strong professional connections. No matter how talented or accomplished we may be, our careers can suffer if we isolate ourselves and fail to seek support from others. Together, let's learn from Bailee's experience and embrace the value of collaboration, mentorship, and networking to propel our careers to new heights of success and fulfillment.

CAREER HEALTH CHECK 5/5

Have you built a Glass Tower?

Some professionals put their heads down, complete tasks, and knock their work out of the park. The only issue with that is they don't take time to invest in professional relationships that cross their career paths. Here are some questions to help determine if you are a professional that is solely focused on their tasks and neglecting to invest in professional relationships:

1. Do you primarily focus on completing your tasks and meeting deadlines, without actively seeking opportunities to collaborate or build relationships with colleagues?

2. Are you often unaware of what your colleagues are working on or their areas of expertise, beyond what directly relates to your own tasks?

3. Do you find it challenging to recall the names or backgrounds of colleagues you've worked with in the past or those in different departments or teams?

CAREER HEALTH CHECK 5/5 *(cont)*

4. Have you missed out on opportunities for mentorship or guidance from more experienced professionals within your organization?

5. Do you tend to decline social or networking events organized by your company, preferring to prioritize your work and personal time instead?

6. Are you seldom involved in cross-functional projects or initiatives that require collaboration with colleagues from different departments?

7. Have you received feedback from supervisors or colleagues about the need to develop stronger professional relationships or engage more with others in the workplace?

If you answered "Yes" to any of the questions. It's important to strike a balance between task-oriented work and cultivating professional connections that can open doors to new opportunities and collaborations. Later in this book, the building and servicing phases of the *skyscraper method* will be very beneficial to your career success.

The Skyscraper

In the Skyscraper career classification, you'll discover professionals with the perfect blend of exceptional networking skills and enjoying a passionate career. In this section, we'll provide a high-level overview, as the rest of this book delves into the Skyscraper classification in extreme detail.

Those within the Skyscrapers classification possess the ability to weather career storms with ease. Even if faced with job termination, their strong network enables them to quickly find comparable opportunities and continue building upon their passionate career path. Skyscrapers enjoy the best of both worlds: loving their work and being well-compensated for it. Join me as we explore each phase of the *Skyscraper method*, helping transform professionals from a Tent, Glass Tower, or Bunker into a successful Skyscraper.

Next, let's complete the Assessment phase, where we'll focus on a foundational skill: reviewing and updating your resume and LinkedIn profile, which I refer to as your professional footprint. Think of it as your personal marketing tool—a chance to make a strong first impression on potential employers. Your professional footprint showcases your skills, experiences, and accomplishments, serving as your own personal advertisement. By keeping it up-to-date, you can tailor it to specific job applications, emphasizing the skills and experiences that align with your desired positions. Additionally, this process allows you to identify any gaps or areas for improvement in your career journey, enabling you to take proactive steps towards addressing them. While foundational, this stage is essential, particularly if you're seeking to transition your current job into a career you truly love.

Chapter 4:
Update Professional Footprint

Welcome to a pivotal moment of your career journey— a deep dive into your professional footprint. Think of it as your personal brand, the essence of who you are as a professional, distilled into two powerful tools: your resume and LinkedIn profile.

Now, you might be wondering, what exactly is a professional footprint? Well, it is the culmination of your experiences, skills, and achievements—all the footsteps you've taken on your career path. It is the mark you leave behind, the legacy that defines your professional identity.

In this ever-evolving landscape of career opportunities, two elements have emerged as the linchpins of your professional footprint: your resume and LinkedIn profile. These two documents hold tremendous relevance and importance in shaping your career trajectory. They are not mere pieces of paper or digital profiles. They are your ticket to unlocking exciting opportunities, building meaningful connections, and propelling your career.

So, why should you care about your resume and LinkedIn profile? Why do they matter in the grand scheme of your career development? Well, let me tell you. Your resume is your personal marketing tool, your chance to make a strong first impression on potential employers. It is an opportunity to showcase your unique value proposition. Meanwhile, LinkedIn, the ultimate professional networking platform, serves as your online presence, connecting you with a global community of professionals and providing unparalleled networking opportunities. Together, these two components create a comprehensive professional footprint that can set you apart from the crowd.

Now, let's talk about significance. Your resume and LinkedIn profile are not just static documents to be crafted and forgotten. They are living, breathing entities that require constant nurturing and attention. Updating them regularly is key to staying relevant in today's fast-paced professional landscape. When you update your resume and LinkedIn profile, you ensure that they accurately reflect your current skills, experiences, and accomplishments. You demonstrate your commitment to personal growth, showcasing your adaptability and readiness to seize new opportunities. Furthermore, an updated professional footprint gives you a competitive edge, positioning you as a forward-thinking professional who is always on top of their game.

By taking the time to update and optimize your professional footprint, you are seizing control of your professional narrative. You are not just a passenger on this journey; you are the architect of your own success. You hold the power to open doors to exciting new opportunities, connect with like-minded professionals, and position yourself for the success you truly deserve.

Now, let's address the average professional—the one who procrastinates and only updates their work information when they're in search of a new job. But you are not average. You have picked up this book because you aspire to be exceptional in your career pursuits. And let me tell you, the success of the *skyscraper method* hinges on your preparedness for new career opportunities at any given moment.

Yes, you may have a resume already, and you might believe it's ready to be shared for a new job opportunity. But is it truly? A common mistake I've seen clients make is waiting until they're in desperate need of their resume for an unexpected opportunity. And what happens then? They miss out on great chances because by the time they have revised and prepared their resume, the opportunity has slipped through their fingers.

So, my friend, I implore you to take this foundational step seriously. Don't rush through it or treat it as an afterthought. Your next dream job could be waiting for you, and you must be prepared to seize it at a moment's notice. Imagine if an executive hiring for your dream job requests your resume before the day's end, eager to pitch you to their manager. Will you be ready? Will you make a lasting impression by promptly sending it over? Or will days pass before you respond, jeopardizing your chances and your professional connection with this executive?

And let's not forget about LinkedIn—a platform where recruiters are constantly searching for new talent. If a recruiter from your dream company reviews your outdated LinkedIn profile, you could miss out on a golden opportunity simply because you didn't take a few minutes to update it. They won't see the full picture of your capabilities, and negative assumptions may be made about your future work potential. Will they dismiss your profile altogether? Or will they interview you and question the gaps they see? How many fantastic job opportunities are slipping through your fingers because of this oversight?

But fear not, my friend. Both scenarios are avoidable if you commit to a periodic refresh of your work history, ensuring your resume and LinkedIn profile remain up to date and in sync with your current skills, experiences, and accomplishments. Don't let complacency or procrastination hinder your progress. Embrace the power of your professional footprint and let it propel you toward the extraordinary career you desire.

To get into the details of how to update your professional footprint. Our Resume and LinkedIn checklist dive deep into the art of crafting a compelling resume and creating an engaging LinkedIn profile. It shares strategies, tips, and best practices that will elevate your professional footprint. Your future self will thank you for the investment you make in shaping your professional destiny.

A Professional Footprint Review

Before I unveil the invaluable insights I've gained from my experiences as a talent recruiter, let me provide you with a glimpse into my journey. For years, organizations have entrusted me with the task of seeking out top talent at business conferences and school career fairs, leading me to review an astonishing 3,000 resumes along the way. Yes, my friend, I've encountered a myriad of resumes—from the impressive to the puzzling, and everything in between.

This unique vantage point has equipped me with the discerning eyes of an HR recruiter, enabling me to curate the ultimate skyscraper resume and LinkedIn checklist. Along this journey, I made some surprising discoveries. You would be astonished at the number of individuals who overlooked the basic step of running a simple spell check on their resumes. But fear not, for I am here to arm you with the indispensable tools to ensure that your resume shines as a beacon of professional brilliance.

If you're eager for immediate assistance, without further delay, dive into the checklist and explore the accompanying resume sample in the appendix. In the upcoming section, we will delve into my general rules for crafting a captivating resume and LinkedIn profile. Prepare yourself for a revelation of the do's and don'ts that will elevate your professional footprint.

What Should You Have on Your Resume?

Your resume should be a carefully curated document that presents a concise and compelling summary of your professional journey. It should include essential sections such as a professional summary, work experience, education, skills, and relevant certifications. When crafting your resume, focus on highlighting your most relevant and impactful experiences, quantifying your achievements whenever possible. Tailor your resume to the specific job you're applying for, emphasizing the skills and experiences that align with the position's requirements. Use clear and concise language, and make sure to proofread for grammar and spelling errors. Your resume should be visually appealing and easy to read, capturing the attention of recruiters and leaving them eager to learn more about you.

What should not be included on your Resume?

First and foremost, remember that brevity is key. Long gone are the days of multi-page resumes that read like a novel. Your resume should be concise, capturing the essence of your professional journey in a captivating snapshot. Trim the excess and focus on the essentials.

But what exactly falls into the "excess" category? Here are a few things you should leave off your resume:

Irrelevant work experience: While it's tempting to include every job you've ever held, only showcase the experiences that directly relate to your target role or industry. That high school babysitting gig or summer job at the local ice cream shop might hold cherished memories, but they won't add value to your resume unless they demonstrate relevant skills.

Unprofessional email addresses: Remember that email address you created in high school that's a combination of your favorite band and a random number? It's time to retire it. Use a professional email address that includes your name to present a polished image.

Unrelated hobbies and interests: While it's important to showcase your personality and well-roundedness, be selective about the hobbies and interests you include on your resume. Leave off the hobbies that have no connection to the job you're pursuing.

What Should You Have on Your LinkedIn Profile?

Your LinkedIn profile is an invaluable tool for professional networking and online visibility. It should include a professional headline that captures attention, a compelling summary that highlights your unique value proposition, and a detailed work experience section that showcases your accomplishments and responsibilities. Additionally, include your education, skills, certifications, and any relevant projects or publications. Don't forget to add a professional profile photo that presents you in a polished and approachable manner. Remember, LinkedIn is not just an online resume, but a platform to connect with professionals, join industry groups, share insights, and build a strong personal brand.

What Should You Not Include on Your LinkedIn Profile?

While it's important to highlight your professional achieve-ments, there are certain things you should avoid including on your LinkedIn profile. Firstly, steer clear of controversial or inappropriate content that could harm your professional rep-utation. Avoid personal opinions or contentious topics that may alienate potential connections. Additionally, refrain from including irrelevant or outdated information that doesn't con-tribute to your professional brand. Keep your profile focused and aligned with your career goals. Lastly, be mindful of the tone and language you use. Maintain a professional and posi-tive tone throughout your profile, ensuring that it reflects your personality and expertise in a polished manner.

How Often Should You Update Your Work History?

Updating your work history should be done on a regular basis to ensure accuracy and relevance. As a general guideline, aim to review and update your work history at least once a year, even if you're not actively job searching. This allows you to capture any recent accomplishments, promotions, or new responsibilities that have enhanced your professional profile.

Additionally, if you're in a fast-paced industry where skills and technologies evolve rapidly, consider updating your work history more frequently to stay current. Remember, an updated work history demonstrates your commitment to professional growth and keeps your profile fresh and engaging.

Common Resume Challenges

In my experience, I've come across two common challenges when guiding clients through a resume refresh. First, for those with limited work experience after graduating, it can be challenging to add relevant information that showcases their skills and capabilities. On the other hand, individuals with extensive work experience struggle with condensing multiple pages of information into a concise and impactful resume.

If you find yourself in the early stages of your career, don't underestimate the value of including volunteer work, school projects, or extracurricular activities on your resume. These experiences demonstrate your reliability and transferable skills, which are highly valued in the corporate world. For instance, serving as a mentor showcases your leadership abilities, ability to follow instructions, and task completion skills. As your career progresses, you may face the opposite challenge of having too much content. In such cases, it's essential to prioritize the most relevant accomplishments and details while removing or consolidating experiences that occurred more than 10 years ago and eliminating extraneous information like hobbies or interests. Consider adjusting font sizes and margins to optimize the space, and leverage your LinkedIn page to provide additional details that couldn't fit on your resume.

Resume TIP to add space: For blank lines between sections or jobs, change the font size to a value smaller than the actual font size used for the text. (i.e., if the text size is 11, make the blank rows an extremely small font likesize 1) This activity will thin the space taken up by blank rows and create more space for your content.

To conclude, reviewing and updating both your resume and LinkedIn profile are paramount for maintaining a strong professional presence. These documents serve as powerful tools to communicate your value, attract opportunities, and expand your network. Craft a compelling story that highlights your unique strengths and experiences, tailoring it to specific opportunities, and keep it fresh and relevant. Remember, your resume and LinkedIn profile are your personal branding assets, paving the way for exciting career prospects. By consistently updating them, you can rest assured knowing that you're prepared for whatever lies ahead in your professional journey.

Career in Action Activity: Revise your Resume and LinkedIn Profile

Walk through the Skyscraper resume and LinkedIn checklist and apply the tips. For the first revision, give yourself at least two weeks to update your work history in detail. Then, ask for feedback on clarity of content from a professional career coach or trusted friend. Finally, create a bi-annual reminder to tweak work history as needed.

Protecting your Digital Footprint

Let's talk about the power of your online presence and the impact it can have on your career. In this digital age, what you say and do online can either propel you toward your dream career or derail your professional aspirations. It's time for a digital house cleaning to ensure that your social media presence doesn't hinder your path to success.

In the past, our personal foolishness did not affect our professional lives because there was no instant way to share our experiences with thousands of people. Employers focused on work experience, interviews, and references when making hiring decisions. However, the internet has revolutionized the hiring landscape.

Today, employers have the ability to learn about a potential candidate's reputation beyond the traditional hiring practices. It only takes a single comment, a controversial video rant, a political stance, or a questionable photo from a weekend getaway to impact a candidate's chances of getting hired, regardless of their qualifications.

Numerous stories abound of individuals who faced repercussions for their online activities. A basketball coach fired for posting a bikini picture on Facebook, a teacher dismissed after coming out on Instagram, a man losing his job due to negative views expressed about Islam on Facebook. This "digital dirt" that can easily be found online can have far-reaching consequences. As a general rule, if you wouldn't want a post to be on the front page of a news feed, then don't post it.

My advice to you, is to proactively manage your digital footprint and clean up any digital dirt. Anything you post or are associated with online can pose a reputational risk and adversely impact your career prospects.

But what if you already have digital dirt online? Unfortunately, it's challenging to erase every trace. However, there are three actions you can take to improve your online reputation and minimize the visibility of embarrassing content when recruiters search for you. Choose the best option or options that suit your situation.

First, conduct a comprehensive search of your name using Google and other search engines. Look for both the quoted and unquoted versions of your name, including variations such as middle name or alternate spellings. This will give you an idea of what potential employers see when they search for you. If you come across negative information, your next step is to request the site owner to remove it. Be aware that compliance is not guaranteed, and legal action may be necessary in some cases.

Secondly, counterbalance negative content by posting positive content that showcases your skills, experiences, and qualities that make you employable. Consider hosting educational events, attending conferences, or engaging in volunteer work. By sharing favorable content, you push down negative results in search engine rankings. Recent information will take precedence, diluting any unfavorable content from your internet history.

Finally, clean up your own social networks by deleting questionable comments, pictures, or posts. This includes any content that may be interpreted as hate speech, excessive substance use, or involvement in illegal activities. You want to ensure that you don't offend prospective employers. If a particular site contains too much negative information, you may even consider deleting your account and starting fresh.

The internet is a powerful tool that can either hurt or help your career. While it may not seem fair that your personal life is scrutinized in evaluating your professional value, it is the reality of today's digital age. On the flip side, the internet can also serve as a catalyst for job prospects by showcasing your outstanding qualities as a candidate. The choice is yours. Use the internet wisely and strategically, and let it be a force that propels you toward the remarkable career you deserve.

Career in Action Activity: Digital House Cleaning

It's possible that you have digital dirt associated with your name and you don't even know it!

Take 30 minutes to search yourself online and scan your social media posts for old, questionable content that you've shared or been tagged by someone in your network. If you find anything that could be harmful, directly or implicitly, to your reputation. Clean it up! Follow the 3 steps to wash away lingering digital dirt that could stifle your career aspirations.

► Phase 2: Digging

Skyscraper Method

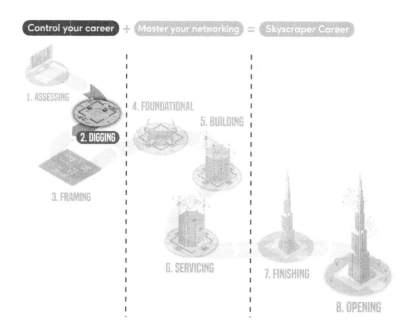

"The deeper you go, the higher you fly." -The Beatles song titled *Everybody got something to hide except me and my monkey*

"This is it," echoed the voice through the elevator speakers as I ascended to the breathtaking Skydeck of the iconic Burj Khalifa, the tallest building in the world. The elevator ride felt like an eternity, a journey that symbolized the pursuit of reaching the pinnacle of one's aspirations. As I stood atop the world, I couldn't help but reflect on the path that brought me here.

Back in December 2010, I embarked on an unforgettable trip to Dubai with my MBA classmates from Howard University. Our adventure took us from Washington DC to Bangalore, India, for an international consulting class, with a 3-day layover in Dubai. And within that short stop, a visit to the Burj Khalifa had become the highlight, a long-awaited dream come true.

As I admired the architectural marvel that surrounded me, I learned the story behind its creation. The preparation and construction of this record-breaking skyscraper fascinated me. Little did I know, the true essence of this colossal structure lay hidden beneath the surface.

Buried deep beneath the ground, almost 200 feet down, lay the foundation that supported the weight and height of this towering giant. To ensure its stability, the construction team had to dig through layers of earth, equivalent to the height of an air traffic control tower or 20 stacked basketball goals. It was an invisible feat of engineering, a hidden treasure that made the impossible possible.

Looking up at the towering masterpiece from the ground, it felt ethereal, like a creation from the realms of dreams. It soared above the clouds, reaching towards the heavens. While millions of tourists visited and marveled at its exterior, few pondered the significance of what lay below the surface. But for me, that concealed aspect held the greatest lesson.

After my visit, I did research and discovered the secret behind skyscraper construction: the importance of digging deep. The quest begins with finding "bedrock"—a solid layer of earth capable of withstanding the weight and pressures of such a colossal structure. Anchoring in bedrock ensures a low center of gravity, safeguarding against the forces that threaten to topple these towering achievements. And it struck me, the parallels between constructing a successful career and building a skyscraper are uncanny.

Armed with the results of your Career Health Check, you possess an invaluable advantage—a profound understanding of your career's untapped potential. You now stand as the master builder, equipped with the blueprints to construct a career that resonates with your passions, talents, and purpose.

To ascend to new heights in your professional pursuits, you must discover your personal "bedrock." This bedrock lies within you, waiting to be unearthed. It begins with self-discovery, a journey to the core of your being. Who are you, deep down? By exploring your areas of opportunity and identifying your passions, you gain the confidence to shape the next steps of your career. This excavation phase of the *skyscraper method* will unearth the bedrock of your uniqueness and reveal your "why." It will anchor you, enabling you to stay focused on a career that truly matters, impervious to the sway of fleeting opportunities or the stress of uncertainty.

And so, my fellow seeker, we now turn our attention to a series of questions that will help you go further into your career bedrock. It's time to reflect, to ponder, and to uncover the truths that will guide you towards a career that aligns with your authentic self.

Are you ready to dig deep? Let the journey commence.

Careers in Action Activity: What are you digging for?

Buckle up,as we go into a set of engaging questions designed to unravel the mysteries that lie within:

1. What sets your soul on fire? Think beyond the ordinary and dig deep into the realms of your passions. What activities or causes ignite a spark within you, making your heart race and your enthusiasm soar?
2. Where do the realms of passion and occupation collide? Imagine a world where your work aligns seamlessly with your passions. Explore how your skills, interests, and values can converge to create a career that brings you both fulfillment and joy.
3. What does your dream job look like? Envision yourself in the role that truly excites you. Close your eyes and let your imagination run wild. What kind of work would you be doing? What environment would you thrive in? Paint a vivid picture of your aspirations.
4. Fast forward to the future. If you continue on your current career path, where do you see yourself in 2-3 years? Picture the destination that lies ahead if you stay the course. Does it excite you? Does it align with your long-term goals and vision for your career?
5. Who can join you on this journey? No one achieves greatness alone. Identify the individuals, mentors, or communities that can support you in your pursuit of career aspirations. Who can offer

> **Careers in Action Activity: What are you digging for?** *(cont)*
>
> guidance, advice, or connections that will help you navigate the path ahead?
>
> Take a moment to reflect on these questions. Write down your thoughts, let your imagination roam free, and allow the answers to bubble up from within.

Remember our opening quote from the Beatles: "the deeper you go, the higher you rise." With our *Skyscraper Method* as our guide, we embark on a quest to touch the very heights of career success. But to reach those lofty peaks, we must first dig deep into our bedrock—the very essence of who we are and what drives us.

This phase is a pivotal stepping stone on your journey, aimed at cultivating a profound and unshakable confidence in your professional identity. It is through this self-discovery that you will gain the clarity to navigate the winding roads ahead, knowing exactly where you are headed. It is through this process that you will construct a career that stands tall and firm, like a mighty skyscraper.

First, take a moment to celebrate how far you've come. Embrace the journey ahead with curiosity and enthusiasm, knowing that you possess the power to build a fulfilling career. Keep your hard hat on and prepare to find the bedrock that will support your dreams, ambitions, and aspirations through a personal mission statement.

Onward and upward, to the realm of passions and purpose!

Chapter 5:
Personal Mission Statement

In the children's story, *Alice in Wonderland*, Alice, while on her journey home, comes to a fork in the road. Unsure of which path to take, she looks up and sees a cat in the tree and asks him, "Which road do I take?" The cat responds with a question of his own, "Where do you want to go?" "I don't know," Alice answered quickly. "Then," the whimsical cat said, "it doesn't matter which path you take."[1]

In our journey of professional development, we often find ourselves standing at a crossroads, much like Alice in Wonderland. We look for guidance, unsure of which path to take. But as the whimsical cat wisely asks, "Where do you want to go?" Without clarity on our destination, any road will do.

Alice's predicament reflects the struggles many of us face when it comes to deciding our career path. Just like her, we may lack a clear sense of personal mission and life purpose. Without knowing where we want to go, it becomes challenging to make informed choices that lead us towards our desired career outcomes.

We've all experienced that desire for adventure without a specific goal in mind, much like Alice. Surprisingly, this lack of clarity isn't limited to those just starting their careers. Even seasoned professionals, with abundant experience, can find themselves uncertain about their true calling. They may have spent years working without a sense of purpose, yearning for

---

[1] Reference: Alice in Wonderland by Lewis Carroll

a deeper connection to their work. As a career coach, my mission is to help individuals find career goals that align with their purpose—an endeavor that often requires expert guidance.

Mission statements are a familiar concept in the corporate world, guiding companies towards their strategic direction. These succinct statements provide clarity on the organization's goals and help investors envision future growth. Without a mission statement, businesses can veer off course and face unfavorable outcomes.

Consider the mission statements of renowned brands we interact with regularly. As you read them, observe the sense of purpose conveyed by each statement. You'll gain insight into the company's long-term aspirations:

"To refresh the world in mind, body, and spirit, to inspire moments of optimism and happiness through our brands and actions, and to create value and make a difference." -Coca-cola[2]	"To bring inspiration and innovation to every athlete in the world. If you have a body, you are an athlete." -Nike[3]	"To organize the world's information and make it universally accessible and useful." - Google[4]

What strikes you as you read and reread these mission statements? Can you sense the organization's purpose? Personally, Nike's statement inspires me to embrace athleticism, and their products have consistently upheld their mission over the years.

---

[2] Coca-Cola Mission Statement and Vision Analysis 2021 - How I Got The Job (howigotjob.com)
[3] What Is Nike's Mission? | Nike Help
[4] Google - About Google, Our Culture & Company News

Just as companies have mission statements to guide their strategic direction, professionals too should craft personal mission statements. This statement serves as a compass, keeping us on course and addressing what we do, how we do it, and why we do it. It encapsulates our unique professional identity and provides clarity and direction in our career pursuits.

As we embark on this transformative journey, let us remember the power of a personal mission statement. It not only guides us but also infuses our work with purpose and meaning. It becomes the North Star that illuminates our path as we strive to make a lasting impact.

What is a personal mission statement?

At the heart of your career development lies your personal mission statement—an articulation of your life purpose, documented for clarity and guidance. It is the key that unlocks the "what" and the "why" of your existence, leading you on a path of growth and fulfillment. For anyone seeking to flourish in their career, completing a personal mission statement is an essential step.

I personally discovered the power of a personal mission statement through the influential words of Stephen Covey in his book, "The 7 Habits of Highly Effective People." In the chapter devoted to the second habit, "Begin with the end in mind," Covey emphasizes the importance of crafting a personal mission statement to overcome internal conflicts. This powerful tool enables you to center your focus on your purpose, develop goals that align with that purpose, and navigate the labyrinth of career choices with confidence. Just as Alice sought guidance from the cat in Wonderland, armed with a personal mission statement, you can confidently declare your destination at every crossroads of your career journey.

Imagine your personal mission statement as the bedrock beneath a mighty skyscraper. It provides a solid foundation that brings clarity and direction to your decisions, actions, and aspirations.

Let your personal mission statement serve as the guiding force that propels you towards extraordinary achievements and a career that soars above the clouds.

How to create a personal mission statement?

Let's dig into the exciting process of creating a personal mission statement. To start, I recommend using a free personal mission statement generator. One that I've had great success with is from Franklin Covey. Head to their website at https:// msb.franklincovey.com/. The generator will pose a series of personal questions, covering a wide range of topics from work environments to life disappointments and influential figures.

Once you've completed the questionnaire, the generator will present you with categories and paragraphs based on your responses. Now, it's time to roll up your sleeves and dive into the editing process. Extract recurring themes and transform the results into a concise, one-sentence statement that truly reflects who you are as a person and a professional. Seek feedback from someone you trust to ensure your mission statement resonates. And don't forget to apply the CCC rule—make sure your final statement is clear, correct, and concise.

Let me share a few examples of one-sentence personal mission statements from my clients to inspire you:

- "To create art that provokes thought, stirs emotions, and ignites change."
- "To champion sustainable practices and protect the environment for future generations."
- "To cultivate meaningful connections and spread kindness in every interaction."
- "To use my skills in technology to bridge the digital divide and empower underserved communities."
- "To advocate for social justice and equality, creating a more inclusive society."
- "To provide compassionate healthcare and improve the well-being of others."
- "To foster innovation and push the boundaries of scientific discovery."
- "To guide and support individuals in their personal and professional growth journeys."

Remember, your personal mission statement should reflect your unique aspirations, values, and passions. Use these examples as inspiration, but ultimately craft a statement that resonates deeply with who you are and what you aim to achieve.

As for my own personal mission statement, it goes like this: "To serve as a leader by living a prioritized life and investing in my leadership skills to improve the lives of others, making God and my family proud." This statement serves as my unwavering guide, reviewed quarterly alongside my career goals to ensure I remain aligned with my purpose. It speaks to my innate desire to help others through career coaching, my commitment to continual growth through goal-setting, and my dedication to prioritize my faith, finances, and family. This mission is uniquely mine, rooted in my core beliefs.

The process of crafting a mission statement delves deep into your core, unearthing elements that you knew were there but may not have fully realized their importance in your life. For instance, during my own mission statement journey, I discovered the profound role my faith plays in shaping my career path. It provides me with strength during challenging work situations and prepares me for demanding workdays.

Most recently, I turned to my personal mission statement to remind myself of the "why" behind developing a career development business based on the *Skyscraper Method*. It keeps me focused on my ultimate goal and grounds me when I face moments of doubt. My personal aspiration is for this business to serve as a career accelerator for you, the reader, and to make my family proud. I can hardly contain my excitement, envisioning the joy on my daughters' faces when they attend my business seminar, seeing the impact of the finished product.

In the realm of personal missions, embrace this process wholeheartedly. Let your mission statement reveal the depths of your purpose and guide you towards a career of immense fulfillment. May it remind you of your "why" and keep you grounded as you strive to make a lasting impact.

When do you use a personal mission statement?

The day will come when you'll be at a fork in your career journey, just like the road in Alice in Wonderland. The decision to choose one job opportunity over another can be daunting. But fear not, for your personal mission statement will come to your rescue, serving as a scale to weigh your options. When you hold your mission in mind and consider the values associated with each choice, you'll naturally gravitate towards the job that aligns best with your purpose.

Now, let's explore other priceless scenarios where your personal mission statement shines:

1. Career Goals: Your mission statement acts as a constant reminder of why you're pursuing specific career goals. Take myself as an example: whenever fatigue sets in during my research for this book, a quick glance at my mission statement on the wall reignites my fire to push forward.

2. Alignment of Work Allocation: Your mission statement provides a structure for how you should spend your time each day. If you find yourself investing a significant amount of effort into tasks that don't contribute to your mission, reflect on why you're doing them and consider whether a change of course is needed.

3. Job Search: When actively seeking employment, align your personal mission statement with a company's vision. This strategic approach allows you to target organizations that resonate with your values, making your job search more fulfilling and purpose-driven.

4. Resume Enhancement: Infuse your personal mission statement into your resume's summary or objective statement. By doing so, you provide potential employers with insights into your motivations and whether you're a good fit for their culture and company mission.

As we conclude, remember that your personal mission statement is the foundation upon which you build your career skyscraper. Once you've crafted it, I urge you to print it out and display it prominently in your workspace. This constant visual reminder will seep into your subconscious, keeping you motivated and focused.

Now, armed with this newfound clarity, it's time to align your actions with your purpose. Let your mission statement be the driving force that propels you towards extraordinary achievements and a career that soars high above the clouds. Embrace the profound power of your personal mission statement, allowing it to shape each decision, seize every opportunity, and celebrate every triumph on your journey to professional greatness.

Career in Action Activity: Create a Personal Mission Statement

Get ready for an exhilarating challenge! Take a glance at your calendar and mark today's date. Your mission must be accomplished within the next 10 days—a first draft of your very own mission statement. So, let's do this!

Here's the plan: block out about 3 hours, spread across a few days, to tackle this challenge. Set aside dedicated time to pour your thoughts onto paper and craft a mission statement that reflects your deepest aspirations. Remember, this is your chance to dig deep, uncover your passions, and articulate your purpose.

Career in Action Activity: Create a Personal Mission Statement *(cont)*

Once you've completed your first draft, take it to a trusted peer for some valuable feedback and revisions. Seek out someone who understands your journey and has your best interests at heart. Together, refine your mission statement, ensuring it captures the essence of who you are and where you want to go.

Next up: We'll harness the passions uncovered during the personal mission statement process and align them with a dream corporate job. Get ready for the passion/skills matrix activity. It's all about exploring where your passions intersect with your skills, guiding you towards that perfect corporate role that will set your world ablaze.

Chapter 6:
Find your Professional Passion

Ah, professional passions—the driving force that ignites the spark within us, the magnetic pull towards purpose and fulfillment in our careers. But what exactly is a professional passion? I think of it as the sweet spot where your skills, interests, and values intersect. It's that exhilarating feeling when you're engrossed in your work, losing track of time because you're so deeply engaged. Your professional passion is the compass that guides you towards a career that sets your soul on fire.

Now, why is it crucial for professional individuals to uncover their true passions? Well, finding your professional passion is like striking gold in the realm of career development. When you're genuinely passionate about your work, everything changes. Your enthusiasm becomes contagious, fueling your motivation and perseverance through even the most challenging tasks. Your commitment to excellence soars, and you find yourself relentlessly pursuing growth and learning opportunities. As the saying goes, "Choose a job you love, and you'll never have to work a day in your life." Embracing your professional passion allows you to turn your career into a thrilling adventure, rather than a mere means of survival.

Unearthing your professional passion is about aligning your innermost desires with your external pursuits. It's about living a life of purpose, where your work is an authentic reflection of who you are and what you stand for. When you tap into your professional passion, you'll experience a sense of fulfillment that transcends financial gain or external validation. It becomes about making a meaningful impact, leaving a legacy that extends far beyond your time in the professional arena.

The quest for your professional passion is one well worth embarking upon. This final step of the *Skyscraper Method* Digging phase involves introspection, exploration, and, at times, stepping out of your comfort zone. But rest assured, the rewards of discovering your true passion are worth the effort.

Why do some individuals manage to find true career fulfillment, while the rest of us are left stretching our heads, unsure which path to take? The answer lies at the crossroads of simplicity and complexity. On one hand, the solution is straightforward—many of us simply don't invest enough effort into discovering our professional passions. We overlook the significance of finding work that truly fulfills us. On the other hand, the job landscape is a vast and ever-expanding universe, teeming with thousands of career options in corporate America alone. In a world of boundless possibilities, it's no wonder that so many struggle to find that elusive career sweet spot that brings lasting fulfillment.

But fear not, for I bring great news and a game-changing solution! To guide my clients on their journey to discover their professional passions, we embark on an invigorating exercise known as the Passion/Skills Matrix. This ingenious activity is my own creation, meticulously designed for those feeling lost in the corporate wilderness. The matrix serves as your unwavering compass, leading you to answer the ultimate question: "What type of job would truly bring you career fulfillment?" It performs its magic by aligning your passions—those things that make your heart sing—with your unique skills, your very own superpowers. For some, the path to their dream career is already evident, and that's fantastic! The matrix will validate your intuition. But for those of you still scratching your heads, unsure of which path to take, fear not! The matrix is your trusty guide, unveiling exciting options for your next career move.

So, let the hunt for your professional passion begin! As we chart the course ahead, prepare to break free from uncertainty and find that career gem that lights up your life. With the Passion/Skills Matrix as your guide, prepare to forge a path to a fulfilling and purpose-driven career.

The Passion/Skills Matrix

Passion: What do you love to do?

In the vast landscape of corporate America, finding your passion is like discovering the key to unlocking daily enjoyment and fulfillment in your work. When you're truly passionate about what you do, it radiates in your productivity and has the potential to elevate your earning potential. The challenge lies in unearthing what sets your heart ablaze. Fear not, for I've crafted a question set comprising eight passionate work environments to guide you on this exhilarating journey. As we review each passion, grab a pen and jot down the ones that make your heart sing.

1. Learn New Things: Are you energized by new challenges? Do books ignite your curiosity? Are you captivated by the thrill of creating something novel? Perhaps learning a new language sparks your fire?
2. Travel: Does the allure of new environments entice you? Do you revel in immersing yourself in diverse cultures? Would you embrace the adventure of jetting off to three different cities in a single week?

3. Collaborate with Others: Does your energy soar in collaborative environments? Do you cherish the camaraderie of working together to achieve shared goals? Are you the mastermind behind planning weekend getaways or group activities?

4. Work Alone: Do your thoughts flow freely in a serene, "library" environment? Does solo work fuel your productivity? When faced with a group project, do you prefer diving into individual tasks and conquering them in silos?

5. Budgeting: Does time fly when you're immersed in a financial spreadsheet? Are you drawn to shows on CNBC or MSNBC? Do discussions about how businesses generate revenue captivate your attention?

6. Coaching Others: Do you possess a natural flair for teaching and mentoring? Do people seek your advice and guidance? Does the positive impact of your suggestions fill you with energy and purpose?

7. Art: Are you a connoisseur of art, drawn to galleries and exhibitions? Do you perceive artistic beauty in the mundane, like rain clouds, cracked concrete, or autumn leaves?

8. Help Others: Is volunteering a central part of your life? Do you actively support non-profit organizations? Are you energized by assisting and uplifting others, especially in a leadership role?

These eight passions resonate with many individuals, and I hope you've found one or more that deeply connect with your heart's desires. Select one to three passions from the list that truly ignite your soul. We'll use these as the vertical elements on the matrix, matching them with your superpowers—your natural skills, which we'll explore next.

Skills: What do you do naturally?

Amidst an infinite array of talents and abilities, each of us possesses unique skills that we effortlessly master. From our early years, these aptitudes often reveal themselves through school, where some subjects come easily while others pose challenges. As we embark on our professional journeys, these skills also come to light during work tasks. For some, creating spreadsheets feels like second nature, while others shine at connecting with customers through engaging conversations. Often, our family and friends notice our natural abilities and frequently seek our help in specific areas. For instance, planning family vacation activities and finding the best deals might be second nature to you. These inherent talents and abilities become our superpower, setting us apart with skills that flow effortlessly.

Now, as we move forward with the Passion/Skills Matrix, it's time to identify your unique superpowers. We'll explore nine different skills, and as we did with passions, take note of any skills that resonate with you.

1. Project Manager: Do you thrive on creating strategies and planning? Did you find joy in completing school projects or organizing tasks at home?
2. Problem Solving: Are you known for your inquisitive nature and love for asking questions? Do people seek your opinion and value your detective-like approach to challenges?

3. Attention to Detail: Does planning meticulously and organizing activities bring you joy? Are you bothered by small inconsistencies and enjoy precision in every aspect of life?

4. Talk to Others: Do you effortlessly connect with new people, even when traveling? Were you naturally drawn to joining clubs and organizations during school?

5. Analyze Data: Do you create spreadsheets for personal use and derive insights from numbers and statistics? Were math and science subjects a breeze for you in school?

6. Analyze Words: Are you skilled at crafting persuasive communication? Do you find errors in documents and possess a keen eye for detail in written content?

7. Public Speaking: Have you confidently spoken on panels or found success in debate courses? Do people seek your storytelling prowess and attention-commanding presence?

8. Research: Do you have a talent for finding the best deals and gathering data to draw meaningful conclusions?

9. Design: Are you artistically gifted and known for your creative touch in paintings, websites, or other visual mediums?

These nine prevalent skills resonate throughout corporate America. Take a moment to identify one to three skills that you possess.

Now, let's merge your passions and skills in the Passion/ Skills Matrix. You'll find the matrix at the end of this chapter as well as in the book appendix. As you find the intersection points, you'll discover job titles that align with your unique combination. Jot down the jobs that match your passion and skills.

If you don't resonate with any of the roles, don't fret. This is a critical moment to dive deeper into your passions and skills. It's imperative to find out what you love to do to move forward with the *skyscraper method*. There are many websites and resources to help professionals find their passions. A good book on this topic is *What color is your parachute? Your guide to a lifetime of meaningful work and career successes* by Richard N Bolles. It contains detailed, easy-to-follow professional passion-finding exercises that go beyond the scope of this book, if you need help navigating that deep dive.

Matrix in Action

Let me share a captivating story of how the passion/skills exercise transformed the life of my mentee, Ben, and propelled him to extraordinary heights.

At the time, Ben was working diligently in the field of risk management. Despite his dedication, he felt a nagging sense of frustration, knowing that something was amiss. That's when he decided to embark on the passion/skills exercise, seeking a beacon of clarity amidst the professional fog.

Upon completing the exercise, an intriguing revelation emerged—financial advising surfaced as a potential match for his unique combination of passions and skills. The idea of transitioning into a new role ignited a spark within him, but he knew he needed validation before taking the plunge.

Eager to explore this newfound possibility, Ben embarked on a journey of due diligence, diving into research and networking. The more he learned about the world of financial advising, the clearer his path became. It was as if the pieces of the puzzle were finally falling into place.

With unwavering determination, Ben took the leap and embraced the challenge of his new role. He quickly adapted to the fast-paced environment, showcasing his natural ability to connect with others through heartfelt conversations. His passion for budgeting and helping others served as the driving force behind his every move.

As days turned into weeks, and weeks into months, Ben's ascent in his new career was nothing short of remarkable. His unique combination of passion and skill set him apart, and he began to make a name for himself as one of the top financial advisors at his firm.

Today, Ben stands tall as a shining example of what can be achieved when passion aligns with skill and purpose. The passion/skills matrix acted as a compass, guiding him to the starting point of his new career path. With unyielding determination and the power of self-discovery, he soared to heights he once only dreamed of.

The lesson here is clear: When you take the time to unearth your true passions and leverage your inherent skills, the possibilities for professional growth and fulfillment are limitless. The journey might seem daunting at first, but with the right tools and mindset, you too can craft a career that sets your soul on fire. So, what are you waiting for? Unleash the power of the passion/skills exercise and chart a course towards a future that surpasses your wildest aspirations.

Career in Action Activity: Professional Passion Hunting

The time has come for you to embark on an exciting journey of self-discovery. Take a moment to set aside dedicated time and use the passion/skill matrix provided with this book. Drawing from the question sets we explored earlier, you should now have a maximum of three passions and three skills in hand.

Think of the matrix as a multiplication table, with your passions listed across the top and your skills listed vertically. Trace your fingers along the intersecting points and discover the potential roles that emerge. As you review the responses, pay attention to those that resonate deeply with you, igniting a spark of curiosity and interest.

Don't be surprised if you find yourself with multiple careers that hold potential. This is fantastic news! Jot down each promising option, and in the upcoming networking chapters, we will identify the best fit for you.

As we venture into the next chapter, we'll build upon the momentum of your discovered professional passion. Together, we will craft an actionable plan that paves the way to your desired career. Welcome the framing phase with open arms, as it provides you with clear direction and a dedicated partner to ensure your success in the realm of career development.

SKILLS: What do you do naturally?	PASSIONS: What do you love to do?							
	Learning New Things	Travel	Collaborative Work	Individual Work	Budgeting	Coaching	Art	Helping Others
Project Management	Product Management, Program Management, Change Management	Consultant- Generalist, Traveling Project Manager	Change Management, Operations Management	Program Management, Inventory Specialist	Balance Sheet Management, Venture Capitalist	Business Development, Employee Relationship Consultant	Marketing Manager, Advertisement Coordinator	Product Management, Business Management.
Problem Solving	Operations Management, Consultant- Generalist	Business Consultant	Risk Manager, Campus Recruiter	Engineering, Information Security, Business Consultant	Portfolio Manager, Financial Consultant	Leadership Development, Executive Recruiter, Risk Management Director	Digital Marketing Manager, Mobile App Designer, Architects	General Consultant, Social Responsibility, Customer Service Rep.
Attention to Detail	Editor, Writer, Application Development	On Site Auditor, Events Manager	Event Manager, Virtual Assistant	Accounting, Computer Programmer	Financial Management, Investment Banking, Controller	HR Manager, Tax Consultant, Leadership and Development Trainer	Process Designer, SEO Manager, Graphic Designer, Techical Writers	Real-estate, Product Manager, Help Desk Technician
Talking to Others	Strategic Analyst, Public Relations Specialist, Career Coach	Event Management, Recruitment, International consultant, Foreign Affairs	Consultant, Vendor Management	Sales, Staffing, Recruiting, Customer service	Product Sales, Sales Training	Career Coaching, HR Specialist, Cognitive Behavioral Coach	Social Media Management	Retail Sales, Recruitment, Vendor Management, Financial Advisor
Analyzing Data	IT Technology, Cloud Architect, Application Development	Tech Consultant, Engineering Manager	Change Management, Information Security, Application Management	Accounting, Computer Programmer, Statistician, IT Support.	Accounting, Investment Banking, Quantitative Analyst	Technology Trainer, People Analytics, Agile Coach	Tech Design, Web development, Supply Chain Manager	UX Designer, Cybersecurity Specialist, Information Security Analyst
Analyzing Words	Social Media Management, Advertisement, Academic Development	Legal Consultant, Travel Publicist	Legal, Social Media Content Creator	Legal, Audit, Risk, Compliance	Securities Trader, Brokers, Compliance Expert, Financial Law	HR, Legal, Auditor	Brand Management, Illustrator, Copywriter, Editors, Authors	Office Manager, Digital Marketer
Public Speaking	Training Specialist, Career Coach	Business Development, Sales Director, Campus Recruiter	Executive Coach, Career Coach	Sales Specialist, Social Responsibility	Financial Advisor, Sales Specialist	HR, Motivational speaker, Leadership Development, DE&I Director	Public Relations, Event Planner	HR Manager, Social Responsibility, Campus Recruiter, Legal
Research	Business Support, Customer Behavior Analyst	International Research	Supply Chain Management, Legal, Information Security	Data Analyst, Research Specialist, Market Research	Business Analyst, Product Analyst, Financial Examiners	Research Coordinator, HR Generalist	Market Researcher, Industrial Designer	Purchasing Manager, Development Director
Design	Social Media Management, UX Designer	Real Estate Property Designer, Creative Director	Strategic Management, Brand Management	Architecture, Product Management, Marketing Manager, Graphic Designer	Product Development, Financial Reporting	Training Development, Corporate Learning	Marketing Manager, Digital Marketing, Film/Video editing, Animators	Product Management, UX Designer

▶ Phase 3: Framing

Skyscraper Method

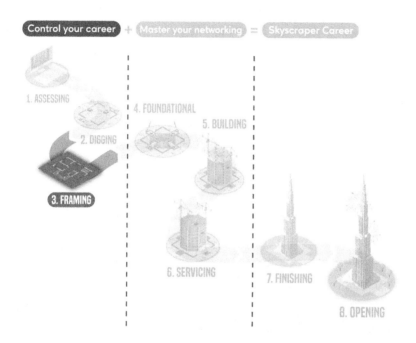

On my visit to the Burj Khalifa in Dubai, we learned about the meticulous process that takes place before the first beam is even set in place. The framing stage is where the blueprint plan of the building begins to take shape. And just like architects and engineers meticulously plan and frame out each floor, you too can apply this process to frame out the next few years of your career journey.

At the heart of the framing process lies vision and intention. Architects envision the grandeur and purpose of the skyscraper, imagining how it will shape the city skyline. Similarly, you must envision your career goals, visualizing the impact and fulfillment you seek to achieve. What does your ideal career future look like? How do you want to contribute to your field? Take the time to dream big and set your sights on the horizon.

Next comes the detailed plan that guides the construction process. Architects draft intricate designs, specifying the dimensions, materials, and structural elements necessary for a successful build. Likewise, you must create a plan for your career goals. What specific steps and milestones will lead you toward your vision? Break down your aspirations into actionable goals, outlining the skills, experiences, and connections you need to acquire along the way.

But remember, framing a skyscraper or a career is not a task for the faint of heart. It requires dedication, perseverance, and adaptability. Just as construction teams encounter unforeseen challenges and make adjustments, you too must be prepared for unexpected twists and turns in your professional journey. Embrace flexibility and resilience, allowing yourself to pivot and adapt as needed.

So, my fellow career architect, it's time to put on your hard hat and begin the framing process. Envision your career future, draft your blueprint, and establish a sturdy framework of growth. Embrace the challenges as opportunities for growth and let the construction of your career unfold with a spirit of adventure. With a solid foundation and a clear vision, you'll be ready to build a skyscraper of success that reaches new heights in the professional realm.

Chapter 7:
Set Career Goals

"Shoot for the moon. Even if you miss, you'll land among the stars." -Les Brown Motivational Speaker

It's time to elevate our ambitions! As you step into the realm of setting your career goals, take a moment to imagine yourself as the mastermind behind a magnificent blueprint, outlining your path to success. You need to ensure you're constructing a foundation that withstands the test of time.

Oh, how I recall the days when my career goal was as generic as a plain white T-shirt - more money and a team to lead. But then, serendipity struck in the form of a book recommendation from my wise sister. *The Millionaire Next Door* by Thomas J Stanley opened my eyes to the power of frugality in building wealth and, more importantly, to the profound impact of long-term thinking on our career choices.

Once that seed of long-term vision took root, there was no turning back. I envisioned myself as a strategic manager, and like a snowball rolling down a hill, the momentum began to build. Pursuing an MBA in corporate strategy became my stepping stone to the career I proudly stand in today. It all started with a single book that changed the trajectory of my life.

I firmly believe that the goals we set today will lead us to the future we desire. As you embark on this journey of goal setting, don't just think about the destination but embrace the thrill of the ride—the growth, the challenges, and the transformation that will sculpt you into the career powerhouse you're destined to be.

Setting goals holds a multitude of powerful benefits that can revolutionize your personal and professional life. First and foremost, it triggers a wave of new behavior, propelling you out of your comfort zone and inspiring purposeful actions. Moreover, goals act as guiding lights, directing your focus towards what truly matters and shielding you from distractions. As you accomplish smaller milestones, you build momentum, gaining the confidence to conquer more significant challenges. Crucially, setting goals aligns your efforts, ensuring that every action harmoniously contributes to your ultimate objectives.

In addition to these advantages, goal-setting fosters a sense of self-mastery. As you steadily progress towards your aspirations, a profound satisfaction of growth and achievement emerges. The journey of setting and achieving goals extends beyond the realms of personal development; it profoundly influences your career trajectory. Remember, you can't manage what you don't measure, and improvement is impossible without proper management. Therefore, cultivate the habit of setting goals in both your personal and professional endeavors to unlock your full potential.

Let's dive in and begin our ascent to greatness!

How Do You Set Career Goals?

Now, for those in the beginner phases of career goal setting, we've prepared a tailored step-by-step guide to help you navigate this journey.

9 Steps to Create a Career Goal

1. **Reflect on Your Passions and Interests:** If you haven't completed the Passion/Skills Matrix CIAA. Take some time to think about what truly excites you and ignites your passion. Consider your hobbies, skills, and the activities that bring you the most joy. Your career goal should align with your authentic self and what makes you feel fulfilled.

2. **Assess Your Strengths and Weaknesses:** Understanding your strengths will help you identify the areas where you can excel in your career. Be honest with yourself about your weaknesses too, as this will allow you to focus on areas where you can improve or seek support from others.

3. **Visualize Your Ideal Future:** Close your eyes and imagine your dream career. Where do you see yourself in the next five or ten years? What job title do you hold? What industry are you in? Envision the type of work you're doing and the impact you're making.

4. **Research Career Paths and Opportunities:** Explore various career paths that align with your interests and strengths. Research different industries, companies, and job roles to understand what opportunities are available. This will help you make informed decisions about your future.

5. **Seek Inspiration from Role Models:** Look up to individuals who have achieved success in fields you admire. Learn about their career journeys and the steps they took to get to where they are. Their stories can provide valuable insights and motivation.

6. **Seek Guidance and Mentorship:** Don't be afraid to seek advice and guidance from professionals who are already in the industry or role you aspire to. A mentor can provide valuable insights, offer support, and help you navigate potential challenges.

7. **Stay Open to Adaptations:** The journey to your career goal may not always be straightforward. Be open to adapting your plans based on new opportunities or changes in circumstances. Flexibility and resilience are key to overcoming obstacles.

8. **Stay Committed and Take Action:** Creating a career goal is just the beginning. Stay committed to your vision and take consistent action towards your milestones. Be proactive in seeking learning opportunities, networking, and applying for relevant positions.

9. **Celebrate Your Progress:** Acknowledge and celebrate your achievements, no matter how small they may seem. Recognizing your progress will boost your confidence and keep you motivated to continue striving for more significant accomplishments.

Remember, creating a career goal is a journey of self-discovery and growth. Embrace the process, stay true to yourself, and dare to dream big. Your career path is unique to you, and with determination and focus, you can build a future that excites and fulfills you. Good luck on your quest to create your career goal!

What is a *C.L.E.A.R.* Career Goal?

Now, when I say C.L.E.A.R., I'm not just talking about your run-of-the-mill clear and specific goals - oh no, we're taking it up a notch with a powerful acronym. You know how much I love acronyms! C.L.E.A.R. stands for Challenging, Limited, Enjoyable, Actionable, and Realistic. When you infuse these traits into your career goals, you're in for an electrifying ride towards success.

Meet Willie Smyth, a 25-year-old retail sales associate, who's on a mission to make his career soar. Now, let me clarify, I chose this name as a nod to the legendary Will Smith - an icon of the 90s culture. So, we'll use "Willie" as our guide throughout this book.

When Willie first started, he had some aspirations - leaving retail sales, making commercials, tripling his salary, and retiring young. Admirable, but managing and measuring these goals? That's a whole different ball game. When he became my client, I introduced him to the C.L.E.A.R. goal-setting approach, and together, we reshaped his vision. Now, he's aiming to become a Chief Marketing Officer (CMO) of a prominent consumer goods company within a decade and promote healthy food options to inner-city children. See the difference? Now we have a long-term goal rooted in passion and linked to Willie's aspirations.

But we don't stop there, oh no! We worked backward to create a C.L.E.A.R. short-term goal: within 12 months, Willie aspired to land a marketing associate role at a consumer goods company. Now that's an obtainable path that excites him, and he's got a measurable way to hold himself accountable.

This goal-setting approach is a game-changer. It ensures that your aspirations are not just dreams floating in the ether but grounded in reality and something you genuinely desire. Plus, you get a roadmap with milestones along the way to your ultimate destination. It's time to steer your career towards the stars with the C.L.E.A.R. compass! In the next section, I'll reveal why each attribute is vital in defining your career goals.

"C" is for Challenging

When it comes to setting career goals, I'm all about going big or going home. And that's precisely the mindset Willie embodies with the "C" in his long-term C.L.E.A.R. career goal - he's aiming to leap from the sales floor to the hallowed halls of the C-Suite in a major corporation.

Landing a spot in the coveted C-suite is no walk in the park; it's an audacious challenge that demands a unique blend of skills, experience, and unwavering determination. The competition at this level is fierce, with countless talented contenders vying for those top executive positions. Climbing the corporate ladder necessitates consistent excellence, a proven track record of tangible results, and the prowess to navigate complex business landscapes while exuding exceptional leadership and strategic vision. Let's not forget the weight of responsibility and expectations that come with the C-suite territory, making this journey a demanding and rigorous odyssey to reach the pinnacle of leadership.

I can't help but reminisce about my own journey as an 18-year-old summer intern, hailing from the streets of Brownsville, Brooklyn, NY - a neighborhood known for its struggles. The odds of making it into corporate America seemed insurmountable, akin to living in a foreign land. But that summer experience in the corporate world left me hungry for more. And so, my very first career goal was born - securing a full-time role in the finance division of that company. The challenge was real, given my limited financial experience, but with laser focus and sheer determination, I achieved that goal in a mere three years.

The lesson here is crystal clear, my friends - when it comes to setting your goals, don't hold back. Push your limits and dream big. Believe that anything is achievable and write down those audacious aspirations. You might not have the entire path to success mapped out just yet, but when you have the courage to believe it's possible, you'll craft a realistic plan to get there. That's where the *Skyscraper Method* comes into play. Your plan may span several years and require strategic thinking, but with unyielding determination, you can reach the career of your dreams.

What are your no-holds-barred career goals for the next five years? The next ten years? Is it that promotion to Director or Vice President? Earning your MBA or PhD? Write it all down, and together, we'll unravel the roadmap to making those dreams a reality. No challenge is too great when you dare to dream big.

"L" is for Limited

A crucial element of setting career goals is putting a deadline on your aspirations. Yes, you heard that right - career goals should have a limited duration and difficulty. They should be bound by a defined start and endpoint, and most importantly, they must be realistically achievable. Let's dive into why this limited approach is a game-changer for your career journey.

With a clear end date in mind, you'll embark on your career goals with purpose and determination. This finite time frame becomes a beacon, guiding your actions and decisions at a steady pace. You'll find yourself navigating through the challenges with unwavering focus, knowing that the clock is ticking, and progress awaits on the horizon.

When you omit a specific deadline from your career goals, the urgency to take action diminishes, and complacency settles in. Things tend to linger in the realm of "someday" and "maybe." It becomes all too easy to procrastinate, tomorrow often turns into weeks, months, and even years. Without that clear sense of direction, you'll find yourself lacking the laser focus needed to overcome obstacles and conquer challenges.

The beauty of a limited career goal lies in the ability to craft milestones along the way. These milestones become your steppingstones to the ultimate triumph. Think of them as markers of progress, each one bringing you closer to the summit of success.

Now, let's take our buddy Willie as an example. He set a time limit of 10 years to conquer his long-term goal of becoming a Chief Marketing Officer. This not only gives him a clear endpoint but also allows him to work backward and craft actionable mid-term and short-term goals. It's like having a roadmap for his career journey, where each stage serves a purpose in reaching the destination.

So, don't underestimate the power of limitations in your career goals. Embrace the notion of setting a deadline and watch as it transforms your approach to achieving greatness. This isn't about restriction; it's about strategic focus and maximizing your potential. With a limited duration and difficulty, your career goals become attainable, tangible, and oh-so-thrilling to pursue. Are you ready? The clock is ticking, and greatness awaits!

"E" is for Enjoyable

The magic ingredient that turns career goals into something extraordinary is the sheer enjoyment of the journey. That's right, when you set your sights on a goal that's deeply connected to your passions, the path ahead becomes an exhilarating adventure. You might not always have a crystal-clear picture of your passions, but fear not, because your emotions hold the key.

Listen to your internal guidance system; it's a powerful compass we all have, that guides you towards what lights up your soul. Pay attention to those signals, like the sense of satisfaction and joy at the end of a task you love, or the anxious flutter before starting something that doesn't resonate with you. Trust these feelings, and you'll gain the intuition to discern the activities to embrace and the ones to avoid.

The truth is, your career goals should lead you down a path that aligns with what your internal guidance system finds enjoyable. I've experienced this firsthand in my early career, where I found myself in a risk management role that left me feeling unfulfilled and disengaged. But then, like a beacon of light, I stumbled upon the Transformation team. My heart skipped a beat, and a genuine excitement surged within me. The work they were doing fed my desires to create new products and improve the lives of customers.

With this newfound clarity, I privately set a goal to join that team one day. But it wasn't until I mustered the courage to share my passion publicly that the real magic happened. A mentor encouraged me to voice my aspirations, and lo and behold, the floodgates opened. My mentor connected me with colleagues in the Transformation team, and within a mere six months, I found myself in that exhilarating space.

So, let this be your guiding principle - seek out activities that bring you joy and make your internal guidance system dance with excitement. Include these passions in your career goals, for it's this enjoyment that fuels the fire of your journey. Don't be afraid to share your desires with the world, for when you do, remarkable opportunities may emerge, leading you to a career that's both fulfilling and enjoyable.

In the journey of our friend Willie, we unraveled the perfect career fit through the Passion/Skill matrix exercise. You see, Willie's heart was drawn to art, a passion that ignites his soul, along with a profound desire to help others. But that's not all; he possesses a natural talent for project management, a skill that sets him apart.

As we dug into the depths of these passions and skills, we stumbled upon a revelation - Marketing Management was the sweet spot for our ambitious Willie. A role that blends art, helping others, and project management into a harmonious symphony of fulfillment.

We pondered, "Who would Willie love to impact as a marketing manager?" And the undeniable answer emerged - promoting healthy food options to inner city children, a cause deeply rooted in his personal journey. Growing up in a neighborhood with limited access to nutritious choices, this mission resonated with him on a profound level - an opportunity to make a tangible difference and pave the way for a brighter, healthier future.

When you align your passions and skills with a purpose that sets your heart ablaze, the possibilities are limitless.

"A" is for Actionable

In the pursuit of career goals, the key is to make them actionable - goals that can be broken down into smaller, manageable steps leading to a grand victory. You see, an actionable career goal is like a roadmap, a step-by-step plan that prevents overwhelm and guides you towards success.

One of my absolute favorite books on taking action is *"The One Thing: The Surprisingly Simple Truth Behind Extraordinary Results"* by Gary Keller. Oh, it's a gem! Keller shares a powerful process to exceed any ultimate goal by focusing on a single task and seeing it through to completion.

So here's the tip I'm passing on to you as you craft your career goals - start with that audacious long-term dream and work your way backward. Picture it like a "domino effect," just as knocking down one domino sets off a chain reaction, leading to thousands more falling in line until completion. Similarly, achieving one task can set off a chain reaction, propelling you closer to your ultimate goal. It's all about planning sequential goals, each one building momentum towards that grand prize.

Now, let me give you a vivid example of the domino effect in action - Willie Smyth is aspiring to be the Chief Marketing Officer of a consumer goods company. Working backward like Keller suggests, here's how his career goals might look:

- 10-Year Goal: Become a Chief Marketing Officer (CMO) for a consumer goods company Question: What ONE thing can I do in three years to set myself on the path to my long-term goal?
- 3-Year Goal: Obtain a marketing leadership role at a consumer goods company Question: What ONE thing can I do by the end of this year to align with my short-term goal?
- 1-Year Goal: Secure a marketing associate role at a consumer goods company Question: What ONE thing can I do in six months to align with my annual goal?
- 6-Month Goal: Apply to roles at consumer goods companies referred by my network Question: What ONE thing can I do in three months to align with my 6-month goal?
- 3-Month Goal: Meet with five managers working in consumer goods Question: What ONE thing can I do this month to align with my 3-month goal?
- This Month Goal: List contact information of five managers in the consumer goods field Question: What ONE thing can I do TODAY to align with my 1-month goal?
- Today's Goal: Connect with one professional in the consumer goods field on LinkedIn

So there you have it, the domino effect in all its glory. Set actionable career goals, take that first step, and watch as the chain reaction leads you closer and closer to the career of your dreams. Embrace the power of planning and focus, and let each small action become a giant leap towards extraordinary results.

"R" is for Realistic

Setting an ambitious yet realistic career goal increases your chances of success. But what does it truly mean to have realistic career goals? Simply put, realistic career goals are attainable and within the realm of possibility, given your current circumstances, skills, and resources. They strike a balance between ambition and feasibility, making them tangible and achievable within a reasonable timeframe.

Now, you might wonder, "How can I ensure my career goals are realistic?" First and foremost, take an honest assessment of your current skills, experiences, and qualifications. Align your goals with your current abilities, while still leaving room for growth and development. Setting goals that require a sudden leap without considering your starting point can lead to frustration and discouragement.

Next, take stock of the resources available to you - be it time, finances, or support. Realistic career goals take into account the practicalities of life, acknowledging the potential limitations and leveraging available opportunities to propel you forward.

Finally, seeking guidance and advice from mentors or professionals in your desired field is also invaluable. Engaging in open conversations and networking can provide insights and a realistic view of the challenges and requirements ahead.

Here's a few questions to consider if your career goal is realistic:

- Do you have time to reach your goal?
- Are you committed to the goal?
- Do you have all the knowledge you need to reach your goal?
- Are there any skills you have to learn to achieve that goal?
- Do you have the funding to reach your goal?
- Do you have the support needed to reach your goal?

In our illustration, Willie's short-term goal of securing a marketing associate role in a consumer goods company within 12 months is not only realistic but also aligns perfectly with his natural skills and abilities. As fate would have it, he possesses the resources to connect with consumer goods managers, ample time to pursue this objective, and, of course, the invaluable guidance I'm providing to ensure he achieves his goal.

You see, the beauty of setting realistic goals is that they are not mere wishes; they are tangible steps towards your grand vision. Willie's short-term goal is well within his grasp, allowing him to build the foundation for his dream career in a consumer goods company.

With his natural skills serving as a strong foundation, his interactions with consumer goods managers become steps towards the achievement of his goal. And with time on his side, he can confidently pursue this endeavor without feeling rushed or overwhelmed.

But let us not forget the power of guidance and support. With me by his side, Willie has a trusted mentor to lean on, providing insights, wisdom, and encouragement throughout his journey.

Remember, there's nothing wrong with dreaming big, but making your career goals realistic ensures you set yourself up for success.

Congratulations, for unlocking the secrets to crafting C.L.E.A.R. goals - goals that are Challenging, Limited, Emotional, Actionable, and Realistic. You've embarked on a journey of self-discovery, aligning your passions and skills with purpose, and charting a course towards greatness.

As you reflect on the chapter's teachings, remember that setting C.L.E.A.R. Career goals are not a one-time event but a continuous process. Allow your goals to evolve as you grow and learn, staying true to your authentic self and the vision you hold dear.

Career in Action Activity: Create your own C.L.E.A.R Career Goal

Now, armed with the power of the C.L.E.A.R. framework, craft a goal that resonates with your heart and aligns with your unique abilities. Challenge yourself to dream big, yet keep it rooted in reality, ensuring it's within your grasp. Leverage your passion/skills matrix results to document the role you desire. Remember, this is not just a goal; it's your roadmap to greatness, a blueprint that will guide you towards a fulfilling and purpose-driven career.

As you pen down your C.L.E.A.R. career goal, let your passion ignite the words, and let your determination infuse them with power. And once you've written it down, take a moment to envision the journey ahead, knowing that each step you take will lead you closer to the destination you desire.

Now, I invite you to take the final step of the framing phase - securing an accountability partner. In the upcoming chapter, we'll cover the power of collaboration and support on your journey towards achieving those magnificent career goals you've set. An accountability partner will be your anchor, your confidant, and your cheerleader, holding you steadfast on the path to success. Prepare to forge a bond that will drive you forward, to overcome challenges, and to celebrate victories together.

Chapter 8:
Secure an Accountability Partner

In the pursuit of our career goals, it's all too easy to become trapped in our own limited perspective. Just like the young wrestler who was frustrated with his coach's instructions, we often think we know what's best for ourselves and that we should handle our career advancement alone. But let's take a step back and remember the wrestler's lesson.

The wrestler's father wisely pointed out that the coach had a different point of view from outside the ring, one that allowed him to see the son's blind spots and strategize to beat the opponent. Similarly, in our professional journeys, we tend to focus solely on the challenges and obstacles we encounter from our own vantage point, neglecting the value of an external perspective.

That's why it's crucial to find an accountability partner, someone who can hold you to your goals and offer valuable insights. Just as the wrestling coach helped the wrestler win matches, a personal career coach, or in this case, an accountability partner (AP), can guide you towards success.

Experience has shown that professionals who go it alone often struggle to achieve their career goals. They may lack a fresh perspective, motivation, and a feedback loop that an AP can provide. Imagine the wrestler without a coach – he wouldn't receive valuable feedback on his fighting strategies while trying to win the match. Winning may not be impossible, but it certainly becomes more challenging, especially when your competition has a coach in their corner.

Now, consider the other job candidate interviewing for the same dream job as you. If they have an accountability partner, they'll not only be prepared for the interview but also have someone to hold them accountable throughout the process. This advantage could make all the difference in landing the job of your dreams.

That's where the *Skyscraper Method* strongly advises you to seek a career coach. Your accountability partner will serve as a sounding board for networking strategies, provide honest feedback on your goals, help you track your progress, and most importantly, hold you accountable to your ambitions.

Having this extra point of view will create a solid support system, paving the way for a more successful career path. So, don't shy away from seeking an accountability partner; embrace the idea and watch how it propels you toward your aspirations. Remember, it's okay to seek help and guidance on your journey to success.

What is an Accountability Partner?

To me, an AP is like the secret sauce that binds commitment to results.

Let me share a personal story. A while back, I found myself in the enviable position of receiving five job offers in just five days, all thanks to my professional network. While it was an exciting situation, I felt the pressure to make a decision quickly and worried about disappointing those who had referred me for the other positions I had to decline.

In times like these, I knew I needed some guidance, so I reached out to my accountability partner, Jim Dallas (Not his real name). He's a wise individual, about a decade ahead of me in experience, leading a massive team of 250 employees. His insight into career transition decisions was invaluable.

I shot him a text, "Hey Jim, let me know when you have time to talk. I'm facing a critical situation at work." And within minutes, he had me on the phone. I explained the situation, and he suggested something brilliant – creating a weighted average score to evaluate factors like base pay, career alignment, growth potential, and managerial style. This way, we could review the options together and make a well-informed decision.

Within 48 hours of that initial text, Jim and I were back on the phone, dissecting each job offer. He attentively listened as I shared my reasoning and scores, but he didn't hesitate to challenge me when he felt I wasn't being entirely honest with myself. "Your energy is scoring this job higher than you are," he pointed out at one point. It was the perfect nudge I needed to confidently make the final call.

Jim's support didn't stop there. He even helped me craft thoughtful emails to HR representatives and the contacts who referred me for the jobs I had to turn down. Thanks to him, I made the right choice that aligned with my aspirations and set my career on the right trajectory.

You see, an Accountability Partner (AP) is more than just a sounding board; they're a game-changer for your career and professional development. They bring objective feedback, unbiased perspectives, and constructive criticism to the table. They serve as your cheerleader, pushing you to stay focused and on track, and they celebrate your wins with genuine enthusiasm. With their guidance, your career goals become crystal clear, and a strategic roadmap forms to reach them, all while ensuring you remain accountable and motivated.

Beyond that, an AP opens doors to networking opportunities, hones your skills, and offers valuable insights to improve your expertise. They help you grow both personally and professionally, making you more aware of your strengths, weaknesses, and areas for improvement.

Time management becomes a breeze with an AP by your side, as they help you prioritize and create a schedule that optimizes productivity. And when challenges arise, they become your trusted ally, offering ingenious problem-solving sessions.

In conclusion, having an Accountability Partner is like having a secret weapon in your corner. They provide unwavering support, guidance, and motivation, propelling you towards a successful and fulfilling career path. So, don't underestimate the power of an AP – they can be the glue that binds your commitment to achieving remarkable results.

Why should you get an accountability partner?

Now, you might be wondering, why is it so important to get an Accountability Partner (AP)? Well, let me tell you, an AP is like having a rock-solid support system on your side, one that can propel you towards greatness and help you achieve things you never thought possible.

You see, we all have dreams, aspirations, and big career goals, but the truth is, life can get messy and overwhelming at times.

It's easy to get lost in the noise, to lose focus, and even doubt ourselves. That's where an AP swoops in to save the day!

Think of it like having a personal coach, a confidante, and a strategic advisor all rolled into one. They're there to listen when you're feeling stuck, to push you when you're tempted to procrastinate, and to celebrate your victories with you. They've got your back, and that's a powerful feeling.

An AP brings an objective perspective to the table, something we often struggle to see when we're deep in the trenches of our own careers. They can spot those blind spots, those hidden opportunities, and offer constructive feedback that can lead to breakthroughs.

Not only that, but they'll also keep you accountable. It's easy to set goals and forget about them, am I right? But with an AP, you've got someone who will hold your feet to the fire (in the nicest way possible, of course). They won't let you slip away from your dreams; they'll keep you on track and moving forward.

Beyond the practical benefits, having an AP is just downright inspiring. Especially when you have someone who genuinely believes in your potential and supports you unconditionally, it can be a game-changer for your confidence and motivation. It's like having your own personal cheerleader, pushing you to go for that promotion, that big project, or that daring leap.

Now, I won't sugarcoat it – finding the right AP might take a bit of time and effort. You'll want someone who shares your values, understands your ambitions, and is genuinely invested in your success. But once you find that perfect match, oh boy, get ready to elevate your career to new heights!

Remember, life is too short to go it alone. Don't let the fear of asking for help hold you back. Embrace the power of an AP, and watch how it transforms your career and professional development.

The story of the wrestler at the beginning of this section is actually from a close friend of mine. When he first shared it with me, I couldn't help but draw parallels between the wrestler's initial short-sighted view and how many employees in corporate America fail to see the value in receiving performance-based feedback. However, just like the son in the story, my friend took his father's advice to heart and started listening to his coach's guidance. The result? He ended up winning the state championship in his weight class that very year.

Now, let me tell you something important – if you want to achieve championship-like success in your workplace, whether it's reaching a career goal, securing that well-deserved raise, or leading an ambitious initiative, you need to seriously consider getting yourself an accountability partner. Trust me; it's a game-changer that can exponentially increase your chances of success.

Here are some key traits to look for in your accountability partner:

- **Invested**: You need someone who genuinely cares about your career development and is willing to make time to discuss your goals and progress.

- **Honesty**: An accountability partner should be some-one who fearlessly provides you with constructive criticism. They won't sugarcoat things or hold back; instead, they'll give you raw and unfiltered feedback that pushes you to do better. If something sucks, they'll be honest about it and then encourage you to rise above it.
- **Committed**: Your AP should be your biggest cheer-leader, someone who's firmly in your corner for the long haul and genuinely wants to see you win.
- **Privacy**: Trust is paramount in this relationship. Your accountability partner must be someone you can con-fide in, knowing that your conversations will be kept confidential.
- **Admiration**: Look for someone whom you admire and respect, someone who possesses qualities or achievements that you aspire to emulate in your own career.
- **Pro-Bono**: This is a crucial point – your AP should offer their advice and support without expecting any-thing in return. This partnership is built on mutual trust and support, not financial transactions.

Remember, finding the right accountability partner might take a little time and effort, but it's well worth the search. Once you have that person by your side, someone who genuinely believes in you and your potential, you'll find yourself achiev-ing remarkable feats you never thought possible. So, my friend, don't hesitate – seek out that accountability partner and unlock the path to your greatest successes!

Choosing an accountability partner

Finding the perfect accountability partner (AP) can be a game-changing decision that sets you on the path to career success and personal growth. But how do you go about selecting the right AP? Let's break it down into simple steps to ensure you make the best choice:

Step 1: Define Your Goals

Before you start searching for an AP, take some time to define your C.L.E.A.R. career goals and what you hope to achieve with their support. Having a vision of your objectives will help you find someone who aligns with your aspirations and can provide the right guidance.

Step 2: Look Within Your Network

Start your search within your existing network. It could be a colleague, a mentor, a former supervisor, or even a friend who has achieved success in a similar field. Someone who knows you well and understands your strengths and weaknesses can be an ideal choice.

Step 3: Seek Shared Values

When considering potential APs, look for individuals who share your values and work ethic. Compatibility in this area is essential, as it ensures a strong foundation for trust and mutual understanding.

Step 4: Test the Connection

Before officially committing to an AP, spend some time discussing your career aspirations and seeking their input. See how the chemistry feels and whether their guidance resonates with you.

Step 5: Mutual Respect and Admiration

Respect is a two-way street. Your AP should respect your journey and ambitions, and you should admire and respect their achievements and qualities.

When you've found the right AP, you'll feel an instant connection – a sense of trust and comfort in discussing your career path openly with them. You'll be inspired and motivated by their guidance, and their feedback will be a catalyst for positive change. The right AP will challenge you to become the best version of yourself and celebrate your successes with genuine enthusiasm.

Conversations about career topics have a remarkable way of sparking new ideas and insights that may not have surfaced otherwise. A reliable accountability partner excels in the art of challenging you when you veer off track from your commitments, all while providing an unbiased perspective. Together, you can explore a wide array of subjects, from acing performance reviews and crafting a compelling resume to mastering the art of networking, acing interviews, building a professional brand, seeking mentorship, and even discussing annual compensation strategies. The power of engaging discussions with your accountability partner can unlock doors you never knew existed, propelling you towards unprecedented career growth and success.

Asking Someone to be Your Accountability Partner

Now that you have a couple people in mind. Let's get an AP on board. I'm here to guide you through the art of the invite with confidence and finesse.

First, set the stage by initiating a casual conversation. Share your career aspirations, your passion for growth, and your desire to take your professional journey to the next level. This lays the perfect groundwork for discussing the idea of having an AP.

When it's time to pop the question, be yourself – be genuine and authentic. Express why you admire their achievements and value their insights. Let them know why you believe they'd make an exceptional AP, and show your excitement about the potential partnership.

Paint a vivid picture of how this collaboration could benefit both of you. Share the potential for mutual growth, the power of shared goals, and how having an AP can exponentially increase your chances of success. Make them see that this is not just about your journey, but an opportunity for them to contribute to something meaningful as well.

Address any concerns they may have. They might wonder if they have the time or expertise to offer valuable guidance. Show empathy and assure them that their unique perspective and support are what you value most.

Make it easy for them to say yes by offering flexibility in how you structure the partnership. Suggest starting with a trial period, where you meet less frequently or have more casual check-ins. Demonstrate your willingness to adapt to their schedule and preferences.

Be genuinely excited about the potential of working together. Enthusiasm is contagious, and when they see your passion for this partnership, they'll be more inclined to jump on board.

Finally, extend the heartfelt invitation to be your accountability partner. Use clear and straightforward language, making it evident that their involvement would be deeply meaningful to you.

Remember, asking someone to be your AP is not about pressuring or obligating them. It's about inviting them to be a part of something transformative, a journey of growth and achievement. And even if they decline, express your gratitude for their consideration and let them know you value their friendship and support regardless.

Once they accept, set up a recurring meeting to track progress. Remember, it's your responsibility to nurture that relationship by meeting on a periodic basis. If they decline, send a polite thank you email then restart the process for the next viable candidate.

Managing an Accountability Partner Relationship

Ah, the secret to a thriving AP relationship – managing those meaningful meetups with precision and purpose! When you get together with your AP, it's all about tackling your goals head-on, with a sprinkle of personal updates for good measure. Let's dive into some essential tips to keep this partnership sailing smoothly like a well-oiled machine.

Firstly, make goal-centric conversations the heartbeat of each interaction with your AP. The objective is crystal clear – discuss your aspirations, share key updates, and strategize the next steps to conquer your milestones. And while you're at it, don't forget to tap into the wisdom of your AP and ask for that valuable feedback that keeps you on the path to greatness.

Next, let's talk about the power of balance. Ideally, you'd want to strike that perfect equilibrium between formal goal discussions and those cozy, informal personal updates. This magical balance ensures your partnership remains strong and resilient over time, supporting each other not just in your career pursuits but also as friends.

After your meeting, don't just part ways and let the magic fade. Take a moment to send a succinct email summarizing the topics discussed and list those outstanding action items. This little ritual keeps both of you accountable and ensures that progress keeps marching forward even between meetings.

Meeting Frequency with Your AP

Now, let's talk about that rhythm of success – how often should you chat with your AP? Well, it's a dance tailored to your unique goals and needs. Some folks might groove to a weekly catch-up, keeping that focus sharp and that accountability game strong. Others may prefer the bi-weekly or monthly rhythm to keep their momentum going.

But here's the golden rule, my friend – consistency is key! Meeting regularly, whatever the frequency, ensures you stay laser-focused and maintain that unstoppable momentum towards your goals. It keeps the fires of motivation burning bright and your vision crystal clear.

You can also tailor your frequency with your objectives. For example, if you're looking to get a new job in 3 months, then checking in with your accountability partner weekly via email might make sense. But if you're looking to add 5 C-suite executives to your network in 18 months, then meeting with your accountability partner quarterly would be sufficient. No matter how often you meet, ensure that it's consistent.

How to tell that the AP Relationship is Thriving?

When you and your AP become a dynamic duo, propelling each other towards greatness in your careers and personal development. That's a great sign you two have great synergy.

So, what does it feel like when the synergy is at its peak?

There's a strong sense of shared ambitions. The bond with your AP is built on common goals and a mutual drive for success. You both understand each other's dreams, aspirations, and the path you want to walk together. This shared vision creates a profound sense of camaraderie and purpose.

Furthermore, unwavering support is a hallmark of a thriving AP partnership. Your AP becomes your biggest cheerleader, celebrating your victories – big or small – with genuine enthusiasm. Their unwavering encouragement fuels your confidence and self-belief, reinforcing the idea that anything is possible.

In addition to support, the AP relationship ensures accountability and motivation. Regular check-ins and discussions with your AP keep you on track, preventing procrastination and maintaining focus on your goals. The partnership provides a powerful source of motivation and reminds you of the commitments you've made to yourself.

Moreover, the thriving AP relationship fosters personal growth and empowerment. Together, you and your AP embark on an exciting journey of self-discovery. You challenge each other to embrace new opportunities and take calculated risks, resulting in remarkable progress and fulfillment.

Last but not least, there's immense joy in each other's success. The beauty of this thriving partnership is that there's genuine happiness in celebrating each other's achievements. You know that your AP's triumphs are an inspiration to you, and vice versa, creating a cycle of continuous growth and shared happiness.

When It's Time to End an AP Relationship?

As transformative as an AP relationship can be, there might come a time when it's appropriate to move on. And that's perfectly okay – endings can be beginnings in disguise. So, when is it time to bid farewell to this partnership?

Separate goals may signal a need for change. As individuals grow and evolve, their aspirations may shift. If you and your AP find yourselves heading in different directions, it may be time to acknowledge and honor those changes.

Secondly, the strength of an AP relationship lies in the connection and understanding between the partners. If that connection diminishes or becomes strained, it might be a sign that the partnership has run its course. Open communication and reflection will help you discern if the connection is still strong.

Additionally, seeking new perspectives may prompt you to explore new partnerships. Sometimes, seeking fresh insights and advice from a different individual can invigorate your growth and open up new possibilities.

Moreover, when the time comes to end the AP relationship, it's essential to do so with gratitude and appreciation. Recognize the growth and support it provided, and celebrate the positive impact the partnership had on both of you.

Ultimately, whether your AP relationship is flourishing or it's time to move on, remember that the experience has been invaluable. Embrace the lessons learned, cherish the growth, and remain open to the exciting possibilities that lie ahead.

My AP Evolution

Personally, I can't emphasize enough how much my accountability partners (APs) have been a game-changer throughout my professional career. It's been a journey of growth and refinement, starting with one AP and now evolving into a cherished accountability group. This group comprises me and three like-minded individuals, and together, we embark on a transformative journey each year.

At the beginning of the year, we share our goals in intricate detail. Each member takes "the floor" for about 45 minutes, to share their aspirations, be it their career goals, business investments, or personal finances. We get vulnerable and lay bare our dreams and challenges, allowing each other to offer open, authentic and honest feedback. This collaborative process gives the presenter three different perspectives on their situation, transforming abstract visions to actionable plans.

Throughout the year, the connection doesn't fade; in fact, it only strengthens. We send a group email every month to check in on our progress toward those goals and discuss how we can stay on track. This consistent communication keeps us accountable and fuels our motivation to strive for excellence.

Incredible things have transpired thanks to this remarkable accountability group. It was within this supportive circle that the seeds of writing this very book were sown. I presented the raw ideas of a career development book to the group, and they offered their candid feedback. And now, *Skyscraper: A proven method to build your dream career* is here!

As I reflect on the journey with my accountability partners, I am filled with gratitude for the transformative power of this experience. It is a testament to the incredible growth that comes from leaning on one another, and it reinforces the immense value of having a tribe that holds you accountable and supports you on your quest for greatness.

> ## Career in Action Activity: Secure an accountability partner
>
> Time to unlock your personal AP. First, revisit the character traits of an AP highlighted in this chapter – the invested, the honest, the committed, the trustworthy, the admirable, and the pro-bono.

Career in Action Activity: Secure an accountability partner *(cont)*

Next, grab a pen and write down as many names as you can think of – friends, colleagues, mentors, or anyone who has left a positive impact on your life. For each name, jot down a few reasons why they could be an incredible AP. Look for those who can challenge you to reach new heights. Use the insights from "choosing an accountability partner" section as your guiding light.

Now comes the exciting part – schedule meetings with your chosen candidates to discuss your C.L.E.A.R short-term goals. This is your chance to see how they can support you, provide feedback, and keep you accountable on your journey to success.

Finally, after careful consideration and heartfelt conversations, you've found your top choice – the one who embodies all the qualities of an exceptional AP. Take a deep breath, the time has come to ask them to be your accountability partner. With the power of your newfound AP by your side, there's no limit to what you can achieve!

Congratulations on completing the first half of the *Skyscraper Method*! You've assessed your career journey, harnessed the power of your passions, and set a clear framework for your career goals. So far, the *Skyscraper Method* has challenged you to work independently, measuring your progress by the work you've done on your own. But now, as we journey forward, we're venturing into the realm of networking – where the method will truly test your interdependence.

With half of the method complete, you're now armed with the equipment to take control of your career and navigate towards your career aspirations with newfound clarity and purpose. But hold on tight because the networking phase is up next, and it's where we'll build the connections and alliances that elevate your career.

Get ready to step into the world of effective networking. In the foundational phase, we'll craft powerful networking tools that deepen the most crucial professional relationships. Embrace the journey ahead– you're on your way to building a sky-reaching career!

▶Phase 4: Foundation

Skyscraper Method

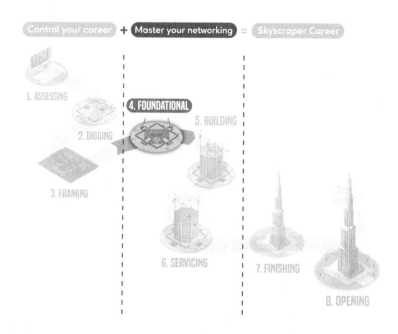

"There are no shortcuts to building a winning team. You build the foundation brick by brick"- Bill Belichick, long-time coach of the New England Patriots, professional football team

Congratulations! You've made significant strides in your career journey, and the progress you've achieved so far is commendable. At this stage, you possess a clear understanding of your career's current state and have a vision of where you want to take it. By crafting your personal mission statement, you've dug deep into self-discovery, gaining valuable insights into what truly brings you fulfillment in your professional life. Additionally, you've learned the importance of having an accountability partner, someone who will stand by your side, supporting you as you work towards your goals. Armed with this newfound knowledge, you are now equipped to steer your career towards success with unwavering confidence.

As you stand at this pivotal juncture, it's time to lay the foundation for your career skyscraper. Just like the Burj Khalifa, an awe-inspiring structure with a strong structural foundation consisting of 100,000 tons of concrete[5] – your career needs a solid base to ascend to extraordinary heights.

In this "Foundational" phase, we'll focus on creating three essential networking tools that will be instrumental in your journey to efficient and impactful networking. Networking with executive leaders can open doors to invaluable opportunities, providing you with valuable guidance, mentorship, and even potential career advancements. These tools will not only aid you in making an unforgettable first impression but will also guide you in nurturing and deepening your connections with these influential individuals.

The first tool in your networking toolkit is the "Hello Slide." This one-slider is a powerful icebreaker, succinctly introducing you and your key attributes when meeting an executive

---

[5] How the Burj Khalifa was built (including design, foundations, cladding and urban myths) - Insight, Burj Khalifa, Skidmore Owings & Merrill, Depa, Guinness World Records - CID (commercialinteriordesign.com)

for the first time. It serves as a concise representation of your unique value and sets the tone for further interactions.

The second tool, the "Snapshot Slide," is designed for use in subsequent meetings with executives. As you build on your initial connection, this slide keeps the spotlight on your accomplishments, aspirations, and growth, reinforcing your professional image and showcasing your dedication to continuous improvement.

The third tool is the "Connection Tool," a structured spreadsheet to meticulously track your interactions with executive leaders. By recording details of your conversations, follow-ups, and mutual interests, you can nurture your relationships with finesse, demonstrating your commitment and genuine interest in the connection.

Mastering these foundational tools will elevate your networking skills to new heights. As you become proficient in their application, you will evolve into a superior networker who can forge meaningful relationships with executive leaders, inspiring trust and confidence along the way.

With your networking toolkit solidly in place, you are now poised to take on the world of networking with grace and purpose. By utilizing these tools effectively, you will create a network of influential mentors and allies, propelling your career to extraordinary heights.

As we journey through this chapter and go deeper into the intricacies of each networking tool, remember that building a skyscraper requires attention to detail and an unwavering commitment to excellence. Similarly, cultivating your network demands dedication, patience, and a genuine desire to connect with others on a meaningful level.

Now, as we lay the groundwork for a successful networking experience, let us move forward to the next chapter, where we will explore the art of crafting a compelling "Hello Slide" to set the stage for your remarkable journey of building lasting connections with executive leaders.

Chapter 9:
Create a "Hello Slide"

First impressions linger in the minds of those we encounter, shaping the way they perceive us for a long time to come. Imagine if you could peer into the thoughts of your work colleagues after they first met you. What would they say about that initial encounter? Did they feel an instant connection? Was the conversation smooth and engaging, leaving them eager to collaborate with you? Or did they simply tune you out after a brief exchange?

As we cover the art of networking, one truth becomes evident: first impressions matter. In the *skyscraper method*, a strong and positive first impression serves as the bedrock for any professional relationship. The burning question we seek to answer in this chapter is simple yet profound: How can you consistently make your best first impression in the workplace?

When I think of making a memorable first impression, an unlikely inspiration comes to mind - Chick-fil-A's iconic slogan, "EAT MOR CHIKIN." This eye-catching message is emblazoned on a billboard near my home in North Carolina, urging passersby to visit the local restaurant. But it's not just the slogan that makes it unforgettable; it's the clever use of life-sized, 3-D cows playfully positioned around the billboard, as if they are writing the slogan in real time. The result? A highly successful advertisement that not only grabs attention but also generates lines of eager customers that wrap around the building and spill onto the main street.

Now, imagine applying the same attention-grabbing principle to your professional life. I propose that every working professional should have their version of an advertisement – a "Hello Slide" – to present when meeting others in a business context. Think of it as your personal billboard, a concise and impactful Powerpoint slide that introduces you to new teams or executives during initial meetings.

The "Hello Slide" is your opportunity to shine, to concisely communicate your unique value proposition, skills, and accomplishments. It sets the stage for a positive and lasting impression, one that piques curiosity and leaves a powerful mark. Much like Chick-fil-A's billboard, this simple tool can captivate your audience, ensuring they remember you long after that first encounter.

By creating a compelling "Hello Slide," you equip yourself with a versatile tool to kickstart meaningful conversations, build rapport, and convey your professional strengths effectively. It's a strategic advantage in the world of networking, where every connection counts, and opportunities lie around every corner.

In the upcoming sections of this chapter, we will explore the art of crafting your very own "Hello Slide." I'll guide you through the essential elements to include, how to strike the right balance between brevity and impact, and how to tailor it to various professional settings.

So, let's take inspiration from Chick-fil-A's marketing brilliance and create our personal billboards – the "Hello Slide" – to make our best first impression every time we meet a new colleague or executive. As we do so, we'll open doors to exciting opportunities on our journey to career success.

What is a "Hello Slide"?

A "Hello Slide" is a powerful one-slide presentation designed to introduce yourself in a compelling and memorable way. It serves as your personal advertisement, showcasing who you are, your family, passions, interests, personal achievements, and professional accomplishments. The primary goal of the "Hello Slide" is to make a strong first impression, grab attention, create connection points, and leave a lasting impact on your audience. When used effectively, this simple yet potent tool positively influences how others perceive and remember you, fostering meaningful discussions around various personal and professional topics.

Research by Medium.com reveals that people remember a mere 10% of what they hear, only 20% of what they read, and 80% of what they see.[6] The human brain processes visual cues far more effectively than the written language, underscoring the significance of the "Hello Slide." By presenting your key attributes and accomplishments in a visual format, you enable your audience to capture and retain the essence of your introduction.

Think of the "Hello Slide" as an advertisement that pitches your unique self to a limitless audience of professionals. It

---

[6] People remember only 20% of what they read… but 80% of what they see | by iDashboards UK | Medium

should contain enough content to stand on its own, even in your absence. If someone were to read your slide without you present, they should gain a clear sense of who you are and the journey that led you to your current point in your career.

When you meet new people, whether they are executives, peers, or teams, your introduction sets the tone for their assumptions about you. A simple action, such as arriving late or early to a meeting, can influence how you are perceived. To control the narrative and guide your audience to a more favorable assumption, the "Hello Slide" proves invaluable. It empowers you to present a well-crafted image of yourself that aligns with your professional goals and aspirations.

Incorporating a "Hello Slide" into your networking toolkit grants you a powerful tool to build authentic connections and lasting relationships. By harnessing the strength of visual communication, you can leave a lasting impression and initiate meaningful discussions that lead to exciting opportunities in your career journey. In the appendix, you'll find a sample "Hello Slide" to guide you in crafting your own compelling introduction.

What is included in a "Hello Slide"?

You've heard about the power of the "Hello Slide" – a dynamic one-slide presentation that leaves a lasting impression and sparks meaningful connections. Now, let's dive into the nitty-gritty of crafting your own "Hello Slide" to make those unforgettable introductions.

The Format:

Let's start with the format. Some organizations might have their own presentation templates, which can be great if you're introducing yourself internally. But if not, fear not! You can still make a splash with your "Hello Slide" by matching its font, background, colors, and borders to your industry of interest. For instance, in my line of work in financial services, I opt for a font that's clean and uniform, non-abstract backgrounds, colors that aren't too flashy, and clearly defined borders. To get inspired, you can check out websites like slideteam.net or do a quick online search to find the perfect style for your industry.

NOTE: Moving forward I'll be showing partial images of the sample "hello slide" from the Appendix.

The Header:

At the top of your "Hello Slide," make sure to include your full name, current title, and, if there's room, your division. Take it up a notch by adding a recent headshot and images of your hometown city and the most recent city you've lived in. You can even throw in logos of schools you've attended, favorite sports teams, or social groups you're affiliated with. These little touches can create quick connection points and ignite lively discussions – perfect for building rapport with your audience.

The Personal Details:

SAMPLE

Interesting Facts:
•Family from the Caribbean (Trinidad/Jamaica)
•Lived: China(Shanghai, Hong Kong, Beijing)
•Host Social Events and Business Seminars
Personal Background:
•2020: BS in Business Administration at Banks College (LA)
•Played College Basketball and Golf int team
•2023: Started Promotional Events Business for Non-

Time to let your uniqueness shine! This section is all about showcasing your personal interests and passions outside the workplace. Let's divide it into two parts: interesting facts and personal background.

For interesting facts, jot down three or four bullets of fun and intriguing tidbits about yourself. We're talking things that wouldn't typically make it onto a resume or come up in a job interview. Keep it light-hearted and engaging. Did you live in another country? Speak multiple languages? Achieve something remarkable? Share your weekend hobbies or favorite pastimes. Let's add some zest to your introduction!

As for the personal background, you can include four bullets of facts that are slightly more serious but still shed light on your journey. Mention your degrees and the schools you attended, any personal businesses you've owned, your family's structure, and any leadership roles in social organizations or volunteer work.

The Professional Details:

SAMPLE

Strengths:
•Relationship management (Sales)
•Process Improvement (Process Design)
•Branding Business Cases (Problem Solving)
Professional Background:
•Sales Consultant: Carmax
•Fashion Design Summer Intern: Ralph Lauren
•Advertising Summer Intern: Ogilvy & Mather
•Jr Brand Manager: Johnson and Johnson

Now, let's delve into the professional side of things. This section is all about highlighting your dominant skills, your value to organizations, and previous work accomplishments. It's the perfect counterbalance to the personal introduction and gives your audience a comprehensive picture of who you are.

Again, we'll break it down into two parts: strengths and professional background. For strengths, pick three or four of your most notable professional skills, which could be related to your personal mission statement or any natural talents you've honed in your career. Are you certified in something? Received recent awards for specific skills? Let's showcase your expertise!

When it comes to your professional background, let's keep it concise.

For clients with extensive backgrounds, it's understandable that you might want to include every detail of your impressive career journey. However, to maintain a clean and concise "Hello Slide," I recommend opting for a table format. This way, you can minimize the font size and list only the most relevant previous jobs, focusing on positions held within the last 20 years. By condensing the information, you present a snapshot of your professional trajectory, keeping the slide visually appealing and easy to digest.

On the other hand, for clients with a more succinct work history, such as recent graduates or those with limited job experience, consider highlighting volunteer roles and internships. This showcases your transferable skills and demonstrates your proactive approach to gaining experience even outside of traditional employment settings. Including these roles on your "Hello Slide" provides a glimpse into your dedication to personal growth and your commitment to developing essential skills relevant to your career aspirations.

The Footer:

SAMPLE

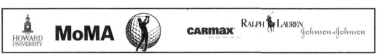

Finally, let's wrap things up with the footer. Here, you'll place a row of logos or images that correspond to the earlier sections. Each image should match a reference, creating a visual reel to complement your words. Include pictures of your family, you performing a skill, logos of previous employers, certifications, affiliations, or images from volunteer events. These visual elements further enrich your introduction, making it more memorable and impactful.

In Conclusion:

As you combine personal and professional details on your "Hello Slide," your story comes to life in words and visuals. By starting professional relationships this way, you connect with your audience on a deeper level, fostering meaningful conversations, and building authentic connections. Trust me; I've experienced it firsthand! Sharing highlights from my "Hello Slide" has often led influencers to share personal details about themselves, enriching our connection and paving the way for productive professional relationships.

So remember, the more you share diverse and vibrant parts of your life story, the better chance you have of connecting with others authentically. It's all about making that stellar first impression and leaving a lasting mark. With your "Hello Slide" in hand, you're well on your way to crafting powerful introductions and building a network of meaningful relationships. Cheers to creating new connections!

"Hello Slide" Tips

Now that you've got a firm grasp of what goes into a compelling "Hello Slide," it's time to elevate your game with some expert tips. Crafting the perfect introduction requires finesse, so let's get into these insider strategies that will set you apart from the rest.

1. Practice Presenting: Once you've drafted your "Hello Slide," it's essential to practice presenting the content.

Time yourself and aim for a concise three-minute presentation. As you practice, take note of the key points and acknowledge specific graphics smoothly. For honest feedback, leverage your accountability partner (AP). Ask them about your pace, eye contact, and whether you're reading word-for-word. Their insights will prove invaluable in refining your delivery.

2. Use Crisp and Uniform Images: Visuals play a significant role in leaving a lasting impression. Ensure that all the images you use are high-resolution and visually appealing. For your headshot, consider investing in a professional photographer for a sharp and captivating image – a warm smile goes a long way! Keep the dimensions of your photos uniform, except for the headshot, which can be slightly larger for emphasis.

3. Apply the CCC Rule: Clarity, correctness, and conciseness are key when it comes to the words and images on your slide. Work with your AP to fine-tune your "Hello Slide" so it efficiently tells your story. Reduce unnecessary details, especially if you have an extensive work background that tempts you to pack in too much information. Remember, you have a limited time to make an impact, so make every word count.

4. Balance the Personal and Professional Content: Maintain balance in your "Hello Slide" by presenting an equal amount of personal and professional information. Avoid giving an abundance of personal details and only a few professional nuggets or vice versa. A well-rounded profile showcases your whole self, allowing your audience to connect with both the personal and professional sides of your journey. I've found that

sharing three personal and three professional facts in my "Hello Slide" creates a harmonious and engaging presentation.

5. Be Authentic: When curating your "Hello Slide," don't be afraid to add details that reflect who you genuinely are at your core. Be true to yourself, and avoid presenting what you think people want to hear. For instance, I include my religion on my "Hello Slide" under affiliations and community service. It serves as a strong connection point with like-minded individuals. Authenticity invites your audience to lean in and fosters genuine personal connections that can lead to fruitful professional relationships.

Incorporating these "Hello Slide" tips will take your networking prowess to new heights, ensuring that your introduction leaves a memorable mark on every audience. So, be bold, be authentic, and let your "Hello Slide" showcase the incredible individual that you are!

Using the "Hello Slide"

You've now mastered the art of crafting an impactful "Hello Slide," but how do you actually put it to use when the opportunity arises to introduce yourself professionally? Let me share with you my tried-and-tested approach that will make this task a breeze and open doors to exciting connections.

When I first started using my "Hello Slide," I found it daunting to incorporate it into my introductions. But I discovered a simple and effective way to break the ice with new influencers. It went something like this:

"Mr./Mrs. X, I've developed this slide to introduce myself to individuals like you. Would you mind taking a few minutes to walk through it with me and offer some feedback on how to best present myself?"

By framing it as a request for guidance and advice, I engaged the influencer in actively reviewing my "Hello Slide" and tapping into their valuable insights as an advisor. This made the brief introduction feel more like a collaborative conversation, making it easier to have. Over time, I tweaked my "Hello Slide" and became increasingly comfortable presenting it in various scenarios.

As you become more at ease with your "Hello Slide," you'll find it a powerful conversation starter during one-on-one introductions. You'll naturally incorporate it into every meeting with new peers, mentors, mentees, executive leaders, or teams. Embrace the opportunity to talk about yourself and your journey, and with practice, you'll flow seamlessly into the presentation.

Once you feel assured, you can confidently tee up the conversation like this:

"Hello Mr./Mrs. Y, thank you for taking the time to meet with me. Before we proceed, I'd like to take the next 3 minutes to share my 'Hello Slide.' This will give you a quick flavor of my background and how I got here today."

When it comes to new team meetings, you can use a similar approach to take charge of the room and make a lasting impression on your new teammates. A great way to start is by saying:

"Hello XYZ team, I am genuinely thrilled to collaborate with this talented group. I have a 'Hello Slide' that I'd love to share. Do you all mind if I take the next 3 minutes to present it?"

Having your "Hello Slide" ready to present means you're always prepared to kickstart the process of executing superior networking. The benefits of sharing your slide with mentors, peers, and teams are substantial:

- Display Organization and Creativity: Your "Hello Slide" showcases your professional approach and creative flair, setting you apart from the crowd.
- Snapshot of You: It provides a quick snapshot of who you are, where you've been, and what you bring to the table, making it easier for your network to remember you.
- Personal Connection Points: It establishes connection points with your audience beyond work, fostering personal rapport and making conversations more enjoyable.
- Primed for Professional Relationships: Sharing your "Hello Slide" paves the way for building rapport with influencers, creating a solid foundation for professional relationships to flourish.

So, take a deep breath, put on your networking cap, and confidently share your "Hello Slide" with the world. With these tips in your arsenal, you're bound to make exceptional connections and set yourself up for career success. Go forth and conquer!

Career in Action Activity: Create your "Hello Slide"

Congratulations on learning all about the power of a compelling "Hello Slide"! Now, it's time to roll up your sleeves and create your very own. Let's get started with a step-by-step guide to curate a captivating introduction that leaves a lasting impression.

1. Personal and Professional Highlights: Begin by listing a few key things about yourself personally and professionally. Consider your passions, interests, personal achievements, and career accomplishments. Take inspiration from the "Hello Slide" example in the appendix to structure your content.

2. Add a Professional Headshot: To give your "Hello Slide" a touch of professionalism, include a high-quality headshot of yourself. Remember, a warm and inviting smile goes a long way in leaving a positive first impression. If needed, invest in a professional photographer to capture the perfect image that truly represents you.

3. Follow the Format: Divide your "Hello Slide" into sections, including a header with your full name, current title, and division (if applicable). Below that, place your headshot, followed by personal details and professional highlights. Remember the CCC rule – keep the content clear, correct, and concise.

4. Seek Feedback from Your Accountability Partner: Once you've drafted your "Hello Slide," review it with your accountability partner (AP). Their honest feedback will help you fine-tune your presentation for maximum impact. They can provide insights

---

Career in Action Activity: Create your "Hello Slide" *(cont)*

~~~~~~

on pacing, visual appeal, and the overall message you want to convey.

5. Tweak and Refine: Use the feedback from your AP to make any necessary adjustments to your "Hello Slide." Ensure that it efficiently tells your unique story and strikes the perfect balance between personal and professional details.

By following these steps, you'll have a compelling "Hello Slide" that showcases your best self and sets you up for networking success. Remember, crafting an impressive introduction is a skill that improves with practice, so don't hesitate to refine your "Hello Slide" over time. With your personalized "Hello Slide" in hand, you're ready to make a powerful first impression and forge meaningful connections on your career journey. Happy crafting!

In conclusion, crafting and utilizing a powerful "Hello Slide" is a game-changer in your career journey. You now possess a potent tool to make lasting first impressions, create meaningful connections, and showcase your unique identity to the professional world. Your "Hello Slide" serves as a personal billboard, leaving a strong imprint on your audience and priming the pump for exceptional networking opportunities.

Remember, practice makes perfect. As you confidently share your "Hello Slide" with mentors, peers, and teams, you'll find yourself getting into a comfortable flow, effortlessly connecting with others and opening doors to new possibilities.

But this is just the beginning of your networking mastery. The next chapter will take you to the next level as we delve into the world of the "Snapshot Slide." While the "Hello Slide" sets the stage for introductions, the "Snapshot Slide" sustains connections in the realm of sequential meetings.

The "Snapshot Slide" serves as a seamless follow-up to your "Hello Slide," providing a concise update on your latest achievements, ongoing projects, and professional growth. This one-slider presentation will keep your connections engaged and informed, ensuring that your networking efforts go beyond initial introductions.

So get ready to dive into the world of the "Snapshot Slide" and discover how it can work wonders in nurturing and enhancing your professional relationships. With both the "Hello Slide" and "Snapshot Slide" in your arsenal, you're equipped to thrive in the world of networking and take your career to new heights. Let's embark on this exciting journey together – onward to the world of the "Snapshot Slide"!

Chapter 10:
Design a "Snapshot Slide"

"By failing to prepare, you're preparing to fail." - Benjamin Franklin, famous inventor, author, scientist, and Founding Father of the United States.

Welcome to our second foundational tool for networking. In the previous chapter, we explored the power of the "Hello Slide" – a dynamic one-slide presentation that sets the stage for making unforgettable first impressions and kick-starting meaningful networking interactions. Now, get ready to take your networking game to the next level with the "Snapshot Slide".

Think of the "Snapshot Slide" as the perfect companion to your "Hello Slide." While the "Hello Slide" serves as your personal billboard, introducing you to new connections in a concise and engaging manner, the "Snapshot Slide" ensures that those connections stay informed and engaged in your ongoing professional journey.

In this chapter, we'll cover how the "Snapshot Slide" sustains the connections you've made after that initial introduction. We'll explore how this one-slide presentation becomes a powerful tool for sequential meetings, allowing you to provide quick updates on your latest achievements, current projects, and professional growth. By maintaining this steady line of communication, you'll keep your network engaged, showcase your continuous progress, and foster long-lasting relationships.

But first, let me share with you the origin story of the "Snapshot Slide". Where did this innovative concept come from, and how has it transformed the way professionals maintain their network connections? Discover the inspiration behind this invaluable tool and how it can elevate your networking prowess to new heights.

The Longest 30 seconds ever!

Imagine the pressure of having just thirty minutes to make a lasting impression on a C-suite executive. What would you want them to remember about you? Your travel plans? Your ambition to make millions for the company? Or perhaps something deeper, more meaningful about the interaction you shared? Let me tell you a little secret – without a solid plan of action, conveying your intended message in that crucial half-hour is slim to none. And trust me, I learned this the hard way during what felt like the longest 30 seconds of my life.

One Friday morning, I had a one-on-one meeting with a senior director at my company. The purpose was crystal clear – to get to know her better, seek her mentorship, and tap into her expansive network for potential job opportunities. We had crossed paths once before, and that conversation was both thought-provoking and promising. So, with my hopes soaring high, I scheduled another meeting, which serendipitously coincided with a chance encounter at the local gym. Fate seemed to be on my side.

In my mid-20s and navigating my first year at the company, I initially believed that networking was all about sporadic chit-chats with business bigwigs. Boy, was I wrong! I soon discovered that this hit-and-miss approach to networking failed to forge lasting connections that could propel my career.

The senior director's schedule was the stuff of legends – crazy busy, and our meeting had already been rescheduled three times. When I finally received a call from her administrative assistant to fit me into a last-minute slot, I felt confident and prepared. Or so I thought. I didn't exactly have a game plan for the meeting, but I figured I could wing it, be myself, especially since we had recently interacted outside of work.

But when the phone call started, her energy was stern, and she was in full "boss mode." It caught me off guard, given our light-hearted and friendly interaction at the gym. Trying to break the ice, I asked about a book she had mentioned during our gym encounter. Her response was swift and curt, "Nothing really new going on in my off-time reading." Ouch! Undeterred, I attempted to pivot and inquire about her work and personal life. But her replies were just as abrupt, leaving me feeling embarrassed and at a loss for words. I started sweating profusely, my mind going blank. With 28 minutes still left, I had nothing meaningful to contribute, stumbling over my words and rambling about inconsequential work details.

And then it happened. The longest, most excruciating 30 seconds of silence in my entire career. I panicked, contemplating whether I should abort the mission or find a rock to hide under. The seconds dragged on, and I could practically feel her anger on the other end of the phone. When I finally regained my composure, I abruptly thanked her for her time and hung up. My lack of preparation had never felt so mortifying.

To add insult to injury, a few months later, I learned that she had taken on a prestigious C-Suite executive role at another company – one that I would have jumped at the chance to join.

But alas, I never managed to reschedule time with her, and her admin never found another slot for me on her busy calendar. I had lost not only a potential mentor but also a valuable connection.

That experience taught me a vital lesson – never, and I mean never, meet with a leader unprepared. And so, the "Snapshot Slide" was born. This ingenious one-slide presentation has been my trusty companion in every subsequent one-on-one meeting with leaders. It has revolutionized the way I present my professional updates, ensuring that every interaction leaves a positive and lasting mark. Join me on this journey as we dive deep into the world of the "Snapshot Slide" and discover how to sustain connections and build relationships that propel your career to new heights. It's time to seize the opportunity to network like a pro and make every minute count!

What is a "Snapshot Slide"? What is its Purpose?

Think of the "Snapshot Slide" as your living, breathing presentation of current achievements and goals. It's like a subtle resume that reveals the latest and greatest in both your personal and professional life. This colorful and concise gem is a time-tested networking tool that will take your career to another level, so you better keep it updated on the regular.

Now, you might wonder, "What's the whole point of this 'Snapshot Slide'?" Imagine having only half an hour to meet with a top-level executive. What do you want them to remember about you? Simple – two things: (1) Are you someone who gets work done? (2) Are you someone who is enjoyable to work with?

To answer the first question, you'll be showcasing your professional prowess through career goals, accomplished projects, and upcoming deliverables. By sharing your work accomplishments, you'll let the executive know that you're a go-getter with big aspirations.

But wait, we don't want to overwhelm the executive with our career ambitions, do we? That's where the magic of the "Snapshot Slide" comes in. We artfully weave in professional stories during the conversation, leaving the executive with a lasting impression of our skills and potential. No desperate pleas for career advancement here – just subtle hints that make us memorable when they need someone with our expertise.

Now, let's tackle the second question – are you enjoyable to work with? Building a connection goes beyond business talk. That's why you'll sprinkle some non-work related topics into the mix – personal hobbies, travel plans, reading lists, or even home improvement projects. These off-the-clock conversations add depth to the relationship and create a sense of ease between you and the executive.

But remember, balance is key! The networking chat should be a delightful blend of both professional and personal topics. If it's all work talk, you might come across as a workaholic or lacking a pulse on office culture. On the flip side, delving solely into personal topics may leave the executive questioning your dedication to your career. Aim for a well-rounded conversation that showcases the multidimensional you.

The *Skyscraper Method* is all about empowering you to craft the career you desire and build the right network. And guess what? With the "Snapshot Slide" in your arsenal, you'll achieve both with finesse. Whether you're seeking a new job opportunity, tapping into the executive's network, or finding a mentor, consistent and flawless use of the "Snapshot Slide" will pave the way to your networking success.

When to use a "Snapshot Slide"?

The "Snapshot Slide" is not just a one-time wonder; it's your networking sidekick for every subsequent meeting with influencers and mentors alike. Here are two prime situations where the "Snapshot Slide" shines:

1. Subsequent Networking Meetings: After impressing with your "Hello Slide," you've sparked interest and established a connection with the influencer. Now comes the crucial follow-up meetings. Whether you're meeting for a coffee catch-up or a mentoring session, the "Snapshot Slide" ensures you make the most of every minute. It's your ticket to showcasing your latest achievements, projects, and goals. The slide keeps the conversation flowing and reinforces that you're on top of your game, solidifying your position as someone to be remembered.

2. Reconnecting with an Old Mentor: Remember that senior director I mentioned earlier? The one with whom I had the longest 30 seconds of my life? Well, the "Snapshot Slide" was born out of that experience, and it can prevent you from falling into the same trap. When you get the chance to reconnect with an old

mentor or someone who guided you in the past, you want to show them the incredible progress you've made since your last encounter. The "Snapshot Slide" comes to the rescue, allowing you to highlight your recent accomplishments and remind them of your potential. It's a chance to reignite the mentor-mentee relationship and show gratitude for their past support.

Remember, the "Snapshot Slide" is not a one-and-done affair. As you continue to network and grow, update your slide every quarter, so you're always ready to present the latest version of your impressive journey. Whether it's meeting with a seasoned executive or reconnecting with an old mentor, the "Snapshot Slide" is your key to sustaining meaningful connections, showcasing your continuous progress, and paving the way to lasting success in your professional endeavors. So, let's dive in and learn the art of crafting the perfect "Snapshot Slide" for every networking opportunity that comes your way!

What is included in a "Snapshot Slide"?

Alright, let's break down the awesome power of the "Snapshot Slide" and craft it like a pro. We'll start with the format and header, and then dive into the six crucial sections that make this slide your networking secret weapon. Check out our sample "Snapshot Slide" in the appendix, so you know what we're aiming for.

The Format: Keep this short and sweet because the same rules from the "Hello Slide" apply here too. Stick to your organization's template or the format used in your industry. For more juicy details, head to the "Hello Slide" segment.

The Header:

At the top, let's put your crucial info, like your full name, current title, and, if you have space, your division or company name. Below your name, let's add a series of images, starting with your charming headshot. And remember, if you've already completed the CIAA (see the "Hello Slide" Chapter), throw in some of those personal images too - city vibes, team camaraderie, and maybe even a recent family photo. This helps your network recall those personal deets about you.

Now, on the far right side of your header, list your core skills or competencies, those special sauce ingredients that make you shine. These should have led to your past successes. Displaying this reminds the reader of your value add, and if they know of a job opening, they can quickly assess your suitability for the role.

Feeling uncertain about your core skills? No worries. Ask your accountability partner, ponder your personal mission statement, and check out these questions:

- What sets you apart from your coworkers/peers?
- What do you excel at?
- What strengths do your customers value in you?

- What do you bring to the table in a company?
- What competencies are listed in your current job description?

Now let's rock those six sections like a pro!

Personal Updates:

SAMPLE

Personal Updates:
- Read: Skyscraper, Outliers, Extreme Ownership
- Played in golf event that raised $40K for charity
- Created back yard patio at home

Here's where you'll briefly mention those extracurricular shenanigans and recent personal triumphs. Keep it light-hearted and current, just like the "personal topics" in the "Hello Slide." Refresh this monthly for max impact. Need some inspo? Chew on these questions:

- What books have you conquered lately?
- Any creative projects on your plate?
- Any personal goals achieved recently?
- Any epic family experiences worth sharing?

Professional Updates:

SAMPLE

Professional Updates:
- Started new role at Bel-Air Technology
- Developed a 90-day action plan
- Added to new project to create social media ads

In this section, highlight three to four bullets showcasing your professional accomplishments and works in progress. Make it fresh and current by updating regularly. Add some oomph with these questions:

- Have you recently joined a new team?
- What projects have you aced?
- Any career goals smashed lately?
- Have you received any shiny awards?

Short-Term Personal Goals:

SAMPLE

Short Term Personal Goals:
- Read: Success Principles, A Promise Land
- Complete Skyscraper Workbook
- Travel: India (Taj Mahal)/Dubai (Burj Khalif)
- Start a new business to teach golf to youth inner city

Short-term goals are those you want to tackle within the next six months. These puppies should be achievable by breaking them down into daily and weekly steps. This section should flow naturally from the personal updates, showing progress from what you've accomplished to what you plan to accomplish. Spark some ideas with these questions:

- Which books are you craving to read?
- Any creative projects to conquer this year?
- A new language to master before your dream trip?
- Non-profit organizations you're eager to support in the next 3 months?

Short-Term Professional Goals:

SAMPLE

> ## Short Term Professional Goals:
> • Complete 90-day action plan
> • Complete new project for Social Media Ads
> • Join the Innovation Product Branding Team
> • Join a Black Professional Employee Resource Group

Same deal, but this time we're talking near-term professional goals. Let them flow from the professional updates section, building on your achievements. Let these questions light the way:

- Any projects or milestones you plan to conquer?
- Eyeing a new job opportunity in the near future?
- What's your short-term C.L.E.A.R. career goal?

Now, let's go for the long haul with those long-term goals!

Long-Term Personal Goals:

SAMPLE

> ## Long Term Personal Goals:
> • Create Financial Wealth

This section should be a one-bullet masterpiece tied to your personal mission statement. Get those gears turning with these questions:

- Dream of starting a non-profit organization?
- Planning a long-lasting family legacy to leave behind?
- Got your eye on a new language to learn?

Long-Term Professional Goals:

SAMPLE

> **Long Term Professional Goals:**
> • Expand and Build on Career Board of Directors

Time to shoot for the stars with a life beyond your current company. Align these goals with your short-term C.L.E.A.R. career goals for cosmic success. Dream big with these questions:

- Eager to boost your earnings to the stratosphere?
- Got a new business venture on your radar?
- Looking to rock a leadership role like a boss?
- What's your ultimate dream job?

There you have it, the "Snapshot Slide" - your networking game-changer that'll keep you at the top of your career orbit! Update it regularly, and you'll be nailing those networking encounters like a pro. Now go forth and conquer with confidence!

"Snapshot Slide" Tips:

You've already mastered the art of the "Hello Slide" with those awesome tips from the previous chapter. Now, it's time to take your networking prowess to stratospheric heights with the mighty "Snapshot Slide"! But wait, we've got some exclusive tips to make your "Snapshot Slide" an absolute knockout.

1. Consistent Branding: You've got your personal billboard ready with the "Hello Slide," and now it's all about maintaining that branding continuity. Keep

things sleek and cohesive by using the same structure and format for your "Snapshot Slide." Remember those "Hello Slide" tips we laid out earlier? Well, they apply here too! Just polish up that stellar format and sprinkle it with your latest updates.

2. Up to Date: Time flies when you're making waves in the professional world, and you don't want your "Snapshot Slide" to be left in the dust. Keep it fresh and snazzy by updating it monthly with your latest personal and professional accomplishments. Think of it as a monthly highlight reel of your awesomeness! No stale news here—your executive connections will be wowed by your ever-evolving achievements.

3. Embody Authenticity: Be true to yourself and showcase the genuine you in every "Snapshot Slide." Include updates and goals that resonate with your core values and aspirations. When you embrace authenticity, your networking encounters will transcend the mundane, and you'll forge deep connections that leave a lasting impression.

What if... I had a "Snapshot Slide" before the longest 30 seconds ever?

Let me paint a hypothetical scenario that showcases the power of the "Snapshot Slide" in action—a technique that could have saved me from the agony of that dreaded 30 seconds. Now, feel free to channel your inner Bruce Lee and adapt this technique to suit your unique style!

Imagine this—I'm about to have a one-on-one call with that senior director. But this time, I came prepared with my trusty

"Snapshot Slide." Oh, what a difference it would make! This slide is my secret weapon, designed to ensure a seamless and engaging discussion, packed with prepared talking points that highlight my successes and create deeper connections.

Before the meeting, I'd be one step ahead, sending the "Snapshot Slide" a day in advance. This gives the director time to review my latest updates and accomplishments, setting the stage for a focused and fruitful conversation.

As the call begins, and we exchange pleasantries, I'd notice her assertive "boss mode" energy. That's when I'd smoothly direct her attention to the slide, starting with light-hearted personal updates. I'd share any new changes or amusing stories connected to the bullets, engaging her in a lively back-and-forth tennis match of conversation.

This structured approach keeps us both comfortable and at ease. I'd inquire about her personal updates, such as book reading, traveling, or family goals. This thoughtful exchange might just soften her initial "boss mode" and pave the way for a more relaxed and enjoyable discussion.

Now, it's time to delve into my professional updates, short-term goals, and long-term goals. I'd emphasize any recent achievements and share captivating stories that shine a spotlight on my work accomplishments. If she has any questions or comments, I'd dive deeper into those topics, seeking her valuable advice to exceed my career goals.

Throughout the meeting, this seamless flow of conversation, fueled by the "Snapshot Slide," cements a sense of rapport between us. We're not just discussing updates, reading bullet by bullet; we're crafting a narrative together, showcasing my value and potential to thrive in my role.

As the discussion draws to a close, I leave with a sense of accomplishment. The "Snapshot Slide" has done its magic, leaving a lasting impression that I am not only a talented employee but also a delightful person to work with—a true networking superstar!

And there you have it—the "Snapshot Slide" technique in all its glory. Follow these steps and watch as you master the art of executing superior networking, a cornerstone of *the skyscraper method.*

The Secret Sauce: The Power of Consistency with the "Snapshot Slide"

Now that you've unlocked the potential of the "Snapshot Slide" and understand its application in networking, it's time to explain the secret sauce that takes this powerful tool to the next level—consistency. The true magic of the "Snapshot Slide" lies in its ability to present fresh and engaging updates and goals at every subsequent meeting with your network.

Picture this—each time you meet with an influencer or reconnect with an old mentor, they are greeted with a new version of your "Snapshot Slide." It's not the same old stale information repeated every six months, but a vibrant and dynamic presentation that showcases your latest accomplishments and aspirations.

Why is this consistent refreshment so crucial? Well, it all boils down to building deeper connections with your network. When your network sees that you consistently bring fresh and relevant updates to the table, it demonstrates your dedication to growth and progress. You become someone who takes their professional journey seriously, always seeking to improve and achieve new heights.

Imagine how impressed your mentors and peers will be when they witness your continuous evolution, both personally and professionally. They'll see you as a driven and motivated individual, someone they'd love to support and collaborate with on exciting projects.

Furthermore, the act of refreshing your "Snapshot Slide" is not just about showing off your latest achievements—it's also an opportunity to discover shared interests and connection points. As you update your personal updates section, you might uncover common hobbies or experiences that you can bond over with your network. These shared interests can serve as powerful catalysts for building genuine and lasting relationships.

So, use the "Snapshot Slide" as your secret weapon to continually strengthen your connections and solidify your position as a valuable and dynamic member of your network. As you refresh your "Snapshot Slide" month after month, you'll find that the benefits ripple out, forming a web of authentic relationships that can propel your career!

Career in Action Activity: Design "Snapshot Slide"

Now that you've learned the power of the "Snapshot Slide" and its potential to revolutionize your networking interactions, it's time to put this knowledge into action. Get ready to craft your own personalized "Snapshot Slide" that will leave a lasting impression on every executive and influencer you meet.

1. Create a Draft: Start by listing your recent accomplishments, both personal and professional. Reflect on your achievements, completed projects, or any milestones you've reached recently. Highlight the successes that showcase your value and dedication.
2. Seek Feedback from Your Accountability Partner (AP): Once you have your draft "Snapshot Slide" ready, leverage your AP. Share the slide with them and ask for their honest feedback. Their insights can help you refine and polish your presentation for maximum impact.
3. Edit and Refine: Take your AP's feedback to heart and make necessary edits to your "Snapshot Slide." Embrace the Bruce Lee Mentality and adapt the slide to make it more engaging, concise, and effective.

Congratulations! With your "Snapshot Slide" in hand, you're now equipped to take on the networking world like never before. This powerful tool will enable you to make unforgettable impressions, sustain meaningful connections, and achieve your networking goals with finesse.

Remember, the secret sauce to the "Snapshot Slide" lies in consistency. By presenting fresh and updated information in every subsequent meeting, you'll build deeper connections and inspire others to do the same. Your dynamic "Snapshot Slide" will become a testament to your dedication and continuous growth.

But that's not all! In the next chapter, we'll explore a game-changing "Connection Tool" that will take your networking prowess to even greater heights. Get ready to learn how to efficiently keep track of all your networking discussions and effortlessly nurture your relationships. The "connection tool" is the ultimate networking companion that complements your "Snapshot Slide" and transforms you into a true networking savant!

Chapter 11:
Unleash the "connection tool"

Imagine having a magical tool that transforms your networking experience from a jumbled mess into a seamless dance of memorable conversations.

You see, as professionals, we dream of building a vast network of executive mentors – those wise leaders who can guide us to prosperity. But managing a growing network can quickly turn into a nightmare without a solid organizational system in place. Ever had a networking discussion that felt repetitive because you couldn't remember what you talked about last time? Trust me; I've been there.

That's where the "Connection Tool" comes in – my networking game-changer. And today, I'm passing this treasure on to you.

In this chapter, we'll unveil the "Connection Tool," the final foundational piece for your skyscraper of success. It's a digital rolodex of networking details, a Google Sheet or Excel spreadsheet that becomes your single source of truth for tracking all your networking discussions. To truly stand out in your networking interactions, you need to remember those key details that others might forget – like your mentor's child's birthday, a recent big business deal, or a book they mentioned in your last chat.

With the "Connection Tool" by your side, you'll glide through the networking world with charm, confidence, and a memory that'll leave even seasoned executives in awe.

So what's the magic behind this tool? Well, it's designed to be your master organizer, your vault of information, and your treasure trove of opportunities. Whenever you connect with someone in your network, you'll record the key details, insights, and action items in your "Connection Tool." No more awkwardly forgetting names or struggling to recall past discussions – everything will be neatly stored here.

Imagine that you're about to meet an executive mentor you haven't seen in six months. Instead of stumbling through the conversation, you pull up your "Connection Tool" and effortlessly recall every significant detail from your last meeting. It's like having an instant replay button for your networking interactions – and it leaves your executive mentor thoroughly impressed.

Now, you might wonder, "Why is this tool so valuable?" Well, it's simple. The "Connection Tool" empowers you to build deeper connections, nurture relationships, and seize opportunities like never before.

By tracking personal and professional details of your mentors, you'll understand them better, making your one-on-one meetings genuinely productive. You'll have the right conversation points at your fingertips, whether you meet monthly, quarterly, or even annually. And that's how you stand out among the crowd – with thoughtfulness, attentiveness, and a touch of networking wizardry.

Get ready to level up your networking game and unlock doors to opportunities you never knew existed. The secrets of superior networking await, and the "Connection Tool" will be your guide. Are you ready to wield its power? Let's dive in!

How to create a "connection tool"?

Let's create your very own "connection tool". To get started, open a new spreadsheet in either Excel or Google Sheets. Customize the table by adding columns that align with your industry and networking needs. Here's a suggested list of headings to consider, from left to right: Name, Contact Information, Role/Company, Frequency, Personal Facts, and Notes.

Now, pay close attention to the last two headings, "Personal Facts" and "Notes," as they are the secret sauce to superior networking. Keeping these details up-to-date after each networking session will be your winning strategy for building deeper connections. The "Personal Facts" section should capture information like family member names, special milestones, or notable achievements. Demonstrating that you remember and care about personal details from previous discussions shows your attentiveness and engagement.

Meanwhile, the "Notes" field serves as your tracker, recording the dates of your meetings and any relevant points from the discussions. This treasure trove of insights allows you to pick up right where you left off in your next conversation, creating a seamless flow that impresses your connections with your thoughtfulness and interest.

To give you a clear picture, let's take a look at an illustrative character, Willie Smyth, and how his "connection tool" might look:

Name	Contact Information	Role/ Company	Frequency	Personal Facts	Notes
					3/23/25: Read a book callled skycraper and recommended it to his whole division
		Diversity and Inclusion Executive		Born in Yonkers Has 4 Daughters	2/19/24: Increase the Diversity 5% in the last quarter. Took his 3rd daugher to daddy daughter dance. Enjoyed a movie called the
Twopac Shakkur	shakkur@apple.com	Apple	Bi Annually	Plays SemiPro Tennis Ran for Government Office In 2012	Juice
		Investment Banking Manager		Recently Moved to LA	4/14/24: Purchased season tickets for the Brooklyn Nets. Gave
Nyomi Campbell	nyomie@gmail.com	USAA	Quarterly	Owns 2 Vacation Rentals	10K for charity for domestic abuse.
					1/27/25: She completed a 5K race. Son got a scholarship to Harvard
		Brand Manager		2 Sons (Mark and Marc) and 1 Dog (Benji)	7/27/24: Help increase sales of new product by using a new brand strategy. Started swimming class. Thinking about getting a second
Hally Berry	Berryh@hulu.com	Hulu	Bi Annually	Loves Country Music	Dog.
					1/30/25: Stated a new project to increase compensation across 3 divisions.
				Daughter owns a photography company	
		Human Resource Executive		Has MBA from Cornell	7/30/23: Volunteers for a race in Chicago and had got approved
Tom Hank	TomHank1999@gmail.com	Visa	Quarterly	Lives in DC	funding for compensation intative.

With your personalized "connection tool" at your fingertips, you'll have the superpower to manage your networking relationships with ease and finesse. By staying organized and attentive, you'll nurture these connections into powerful alliances that enrich your professional journey and open doors to exciting opportunities. So, let's build your "connection tool" and unlock the true potential of your networking endeavors. The benefits are boundless, and your future self will thank you for it. Get ready to make your network flourish like never before!

How to best use the "connection tool"?

Using the "connection tool" to its full potential is the key to making your professional networking efforts truly stand out. As soon as you start meeting with executive leaders, use the tool to update personal facts and key details about them – where they live, family notes, and other highlights of your conversations. This way, you'll always have a wealth of information at your fingertips, ready to be used as powerful conversation starters when you reconnect with these leaders in the future.

Let's take a look at an example featuring our guy Willie Smyth and his quarterly meeting with Nyomi Campbell, the USAA Investment Banking Manager.

Scenario one: Without reviewing any notes prior to the chat, Willie resorts to common networking questions like, "How is everything going at USAA?" or "What problems from work keep you up at night?" However, this approach doesn't make Willie stand out, and Nyomi's responses are equally common-place, leading to a shallow conversation that lacks depth.

Scenario two: Now, imagine if Willie had taken a moment to review his "connection tool" before the meeting. He would have seen that in their last discussion, they chatted about Nyomi's philanthropy work with Domestic Abuse victims and her recent move to LA. Armed with this knowledge, Willie crafts intentional questions such as, "Where do you see the funds used to end Domestic Abuse needed most?" or "Did you purchase any rental properties in LA after your move?". These specific and thoughtful questions elevate the networking con-versation, delving into deeper topics and fostering engaging back-and-forth dialogue. This kind of intentional exchange strengthens the relationship and professional connection, mak-ing the interaction more meaningful and memorable.

That's why the "connection tool" is invaluable for building your professional network. It empowers you with the insights and knowledge needed to create intentional and meaningful connections with executive leaders. By leveraging the infor-mation in your "connection tool," you can navigate network-ing discussions with ease and make a lasting impression on your mentors and peers alike.

What are the results of using the "connection tool"?

The "connection tool" yields powerful results by making "weak" connections with executive leaders stronger. Strengthening weak ties is the process of nurturing and deepening relationships with individuals whom you may have had limited interactions with in the past. By investing time and effort into these connections, you transform them from superficial encounters to meaningful and valuable alliances. Actively engaging with others, showing genuine interest in their lives and accomplishments, and finding common interests or goals to build upon are all essential to this process.

As you consistently use the "connection tool," its benefits become apparent in both the short and long term. Before a networking discussion, the tool serves as a handy reference, reminding you of key details and enabling you to engage in more meaningful conversations. You'll show your mentors that you are attentive, organized, and genuinely interested in their experiences, which leaves a lasting impression. Over time, this consistency fosters closer relationships with your mentors, opening doors to new opportunities and a more enriching network.

On the other hand, neglecting to create or use the "connection tool" can hinder your networking efforts. Relying solely on memory during discussions may lead to repetitive and unproductive conversations, limiting the potential growth of promising relationships. Organization is the key to successful mentor management, and by diligently tracking networking highlights in the tool, you demonstrate your commitment to nurturing these connections.

In my experience, meaningful mentor/mentee conversations thrive when both parties share personal and professional details. The "hello" and "snapshot" slides are tools for sharing relevant information with your mentors, while the "connection tool" is designed to document the valuable insights you receive from them. By using the "connection tool" to recall and discuss personal and professional details accurately, you build trust and rapport with your network.

To execute superior networking and fully embrace *the skyscraper method*, keeping track of networking highlights in the "connection tool" is crucial. Remember, the ability to recall important details from past conversations helps solidify your connections and demonstrates your thoughtfulness and attentiveness. As you continue to use this powerful tool, you'll witness the exponential benefits of nurturing and strengthening your professional relationships, propelling your career growth to new levels.

Who should be added to your "connection tool"?

You might be wondering, "Having a tool is nice and all, but I don't have any names to add to it." Fear not, my friend, for it's time to unleash the power of the mentor hit list! In this section, I'll show you how to brainstorm and identify the trusted advisers who will guide you on your career journey.

Let's begin by recognizing that you already have connections that could serve as valuable mentors. Look for individuals with relevant knowledge in your career interest, those who can provide honest feedback, and those who show a willingness to invest in your growth. Now, let's walk through an activity to help you pinpoint who should make it onto your mentor hit list and why. This list of names will be the foundation to turn those weak ties into strong bonds.

Grab a blank page and consider the following brainstorming questions:

- Who would you like to learn more from?
- Is there someone from your past who worked in an area you'd like to explore further?
- Who in your organization has achieved the level you aspire to reach one day?
- Are there individuals you wish you had continued conversations with?
- Think back to interviews you've had in the past. Who did you have great conversations with, even if you didn't get the job?
- If you needed a job today, who would you contact, even if it's been a while since you last spoke?
- Are there past colleagues or superiors you'd love to work with again in the future?
- Can you recall someone who profoundly influenced your career through their words or actions?
- Who took a chance on you in your past work experiences?

By answering these questions, you'll start to see names emerge that align with your career goals and aspirations. Now, if you're still having trouble creating your hit list, here's another approach to consider. Broaden your scope and identify different groups of people you know, such as family, friends, church members, and coworkers. Review the questions again and jot down the names that come to mind, evaluating whether these individuals can fulfill your needs.

(Quick tip: Diversify your mentor hit list. Don't limit your network based on gender, ethnicity, or background. Embrace diversity, as it opens doors to a wealth of knowledge and enhances your career development potential.)

With your mentor hit list in hand, you'll be equipped to nurture these connections and make them stronger. These individuals will become your invaluable guides, providing insights, support, and opportunities to help you reach new heights in your career. Remember, the mentor hit list is the launchpad for building a powerful and diverse network that propels you towards success. So, let's get those names on your "connection tool" and embark on this transformative journey together.

Strategize the reconnection

Once you have a few names on your "connection tool," it's crucial to go beyond merely collecting information and develop a well-thought-out strategic plan for each connection. This plan should serve as your personalized roadmap for nurturing and strengthening these relationships effectively. Start by reviewing any notes from past interactions, such as how you met and the key topics discussed. Understanding the context of your previous encounters will help you approach future interactions more thoughtfully.

Next, consider the best way to connect with each person. Some may prefer email, while others may be more responsive on social media platforms or through phone calls. Tailoring your approach to their communication preferences shows your attentiveness and respect for their time.

Identify common interests or experiences that you share with each connection. These shared elements create a bond and provide excellent conversation starters. Whether it's a shared hobby, professional background, or similar career aspirations, leveraging common ground can foster a deeper connection and strengthen your rapport.

Moreover, consider what each person can offer in your development journey. Are they experts in a particular field you aspire to work in? Do they have a wealth of knowledge and experiences that align with your C.L.E.A.R career goals? Understanding their strengths and expertise will help you make the most of your interactions and maximize the value you can gain from these relationships.

With this strategic plan in place, you'll approach your networking discussions with purpose and intention. By utilizing the insights gathered in your "connection tool," you'll navigate each conversation skillfully, building rapport, and making a lasting impact. Remember, superior networking is about building meaningful connections and nurturing them over time. With a well-crafted plan, you'll set yourself apart from the crowd and forge professional relationships that will contribute to your success and growth.

Career in Action Activity: Make a "connection tool"

It's time to take action and create your very own "connection tool" – a powerful resource that will supercharge your professional relationships and career growth.

To begin, open a Google sheet or Excel spreadsheet and start making your mentor hit list. Use the brainstorming questions we provided earlier to identify individuals who can guide you on your career journey. These are the people you'll add to your "connection tool" to nurture and strengthen your professional connections.

Your mentor hit list is the starting point for building a network that will propel your career to new heights. These valuable relationships will offer you insights, support, and opportunities you may not have imagined before. With consistent communication, you'll build familiarity and trust, ensuring your network becomes an invaluable asset throughout your career.

As you engage with your mentors, remember to prioritize frequent contact. Schedule meetings bi-annually, quarterly, or as appropriate for your relationships. The more you meet, the deeper your connections will become, and the more they will sustain and enrich your professional journey.

Congratulations, you've reached a pivotal moment in your networking journey!

Now, armed with the three foundational tools of *the skyscraper method* – the "hello slide," the "snapshot slide," and the "connection tool" – you're well-prepared to become a superior networker. These tools will help you leave lasting impressions, sustain your professional relationships, and manage quality discussions with influential individuals.

With the "connection tool" in hand, you're now ready for the next phase of the *skyscraper method* – building your network. In this exciting phase, we'll show you how to put all these activities into action and create a dynamic networking life cycle that propels your career forward.

▶ Phase 5: Build

Skyscraper Method

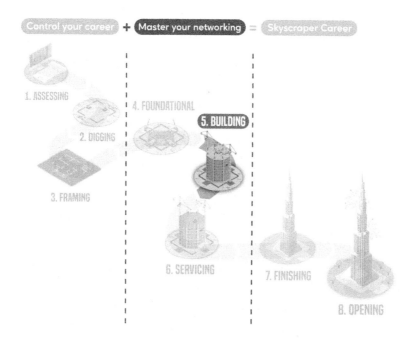

"Networking is the number one unwritten rule of success in business." - Sallie L. Krawcheck- CEO of Ellevest Investments

Welcome to the action-packed phase of *the skyscraper method*: Build. In this phase, we will dive into the actionable steps to network effectively and cultivate high-quality relationships. The word "Build" embodies the essence of taking proactive steps to create and expand your professional network.

Through my own experiences, I've learned that building a professional network is an ongoing process. Corporate work environments are dynamic and ever-changing, presenting myriad opportunities to interact with influential individuals. Whether it's connecting with new hires, engaging in after-work social outings, attending conferences with keynote speakers, leveraging social media, reading industry blogs, participating in board meetings, or exploring other avenues, the possibilities to interact with career-impacting professionals seem boundless. Each of these interactions has the potential to evolve into a mentoring relationship, lead you to your dream career through a supportive leader, or provide guidance from a peer during challenging business decisions. However, the key to unlocking this potential lies in your initiative to proactively develop and nurture these professional relationships after the first interaction.

Before we go further into networking strategies, it's crucial to address a gentle reminder. If you haven't completed the Career in Action activity items that you keep putting off, now is the time to take action. Having these activities completed will bolster your confidence and lay a solid foundation for this phase, setting you up to construct your own skyscraper of success.

Throughout this phase, we will seamlessly integrate Career in Action activities into a cohesive networking system called the "Networking Life Cycle." Avoid the trap of only partially completing some of the activities in this book, as it may result in a career journey resembling the leaning tower of Pisa. Instead, aim for the pinnacle of success, the Burj Khalifa of career journeys. Now, let's roll up our sleeves and begin to build the career you've always aspired to!

Chapter 12:
Launch your Networking
Life Cycle

Welcome to the heart of strategic networking - the "Networking Life Cycle." This term embodies the rhythm of initiating, nurturing, and managing professional relationships, ultimately propelling you towards career success. In this chapter and in the appendix, you'll find a visual flow chart of this life-altering cycle, providing a compass to navigate the uncharted waters of corporate connections.

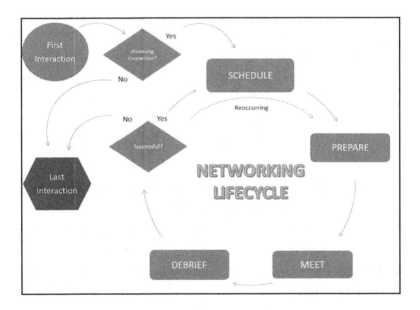

It all begins with that pivotal first interaction, a moment that can make or break your journey. Engaging with potential influencers - be it seasoned executives, revered senior leaders, or inspiring peers - sets the stage for what's to come. Here's my advice: If you sense that this connection won't align with your goals, gracefully exit the stage. But when you feel the spark of promise, that's when the "Networking Life Cycle" comes into play.

Four distinct stages define this transformative cycle: schedule, prepare, meet, and debrief. Each step is a crucial link in the chain, where the magic of networking unfolds. And after the debrief stage, a game-changing decision point awaits: "successful?" This is where you gauge the meeting's impact and decide whether to embark on another round with the influencer.

Now, hold on tight as we journey through the intricacies of each stage. We'll explore the ups and downs of the "Networking Life Cycle" through the captivating tale of Willie Smyth and the transformational influence of a mentor who steered my career to new levels.

The First Interaction:

The beauty of the first interaction with a potential influencer lies in its spontaneity. It can unfold anywhere, anytime, and in any circumstance. What truly matters is the exchange of information during this initial encounter - the pivotal question being, "Does this interaction hint at a potential value in building a relationship?"

Let's follow the captivating story of Willie, who found himself at a young professionals Marketing conference. There, he met the Chief Marketing Officer (CMO) of a consumer goods company, Mrs. Jazz. In just five minutes, they engaged in a chat about marketing to diverse markets. Willie's heart raced as Mrs. Jazz shared her passion for creating strategies to provide healthy food options to inner-city children - his dream job. Though their conversation was cut short, Mrs. Jazz handed Willie her business card. Instantly, he knew that this encounter had the potential to lead him towards a career opportunity he deeply desired.

Drawing from my two decades of corporate experience, I've been fortunate to cross paths with countless mentors who have profoundly shaped my career. These initial interactions with my mentors took place in a multitude of settings, from team meetings and weekend conferences to job interviews, email introductions, happy hours, and even on a golf course.

Reflecting on my early career, I must confess that I initially stayed away from networking. My focus was solely on completing assigned tasks, and I kept to myself, leading to a narrow perspective on my career path. It was my wise sister who urged me to break free from my comfort zone in Charlotte and connect with like-minded professionals. She knew that expanding my network would offer fresh perspectives and elevate my career to new heights.

Taking her advice to heart, I embraced an opportunity to attend a golf fundraiser for the Charlotte Boys and Girls Club. Golf, a foreign language to me back then, triggered feelings of apprehension and embarrassment. Yet, my fear of an uncertain career path outweighed any humiliation on the golf course. With determination, I signed up for the event, hoping to connect with people who could inspire my journey.

On the day of the fundraiser, as fate would have it, I found myself on a team with three senior executives from top firms in Charlotte. Despite feeling like an outsider, I wore a game face and approached them with a lighthearted remark: "Gentlemen, before we get started, you must know - I'm not here to golf, I'm only here for the cold brews." My playful approach was met with warm smiles and open arms, particularly from one of the executives, Nelson.

That day marked my first interaction with Nelson, but little did I know it was only the beginning of a transformative relationship.

Could this be a Promising Connection?

At the time, Nelson was a cigar-toting Midwesterner, twice my age, and overflowing with a friendly spirit. As we exchanged introductions, he couldn't help but chuckle when I confessed my lack of golf skills for the day. Undeterred, he offered to talk me through the basics while we rode in the same cart for 18 holes. Amidst spring weather and cold brews, we shared stories about family, business, and of course, golf.

Nelson's work involved managing contracts between financial organizations and vendors, putting him at the epicenter of major business partnerships in Charlotte. Back then, I didn't have a personal mission statement, a networking plan, or an accountability partner. My career direction seemed uncertain. But the sparks of synergy with Nelson, his golf expertise, and his wealth of business knowledge sparked an insatiable curiosity within me.

By the end of the golf event, I felt a promising connection had been kindled. I promptly exchanged information with Nelson to set up further conversations.

Now, how can you discern if a connection holds promise?

The key lies not in the duration of the first interaction but in the gaps it reveals. Take a cue from Willie's encounter with Mrs. Jazz - she currently holds his dream job, possessing the knowledge and experience he needs to enter her industry.

So, after that first interaction, ask yourself, "What career gap can this person fill?" Are there areas of knowledge, experience, or business that this individual can enrich for you? If the answer is a resounding yes, then forging a networking relationship holds great potential. But remember, once you decide to embark on this journey, tailor the discussions to focus on closing those identified gaps. Set C.L.E.A.R. goals to guide your progress.

The most common reason to pursue networking is to bridge a knowledge gap. When I spent that day with Nelson, I realized I needed to learn golf (personal) and understand the monetary benefits of relationship management (professional).

But it's not just knowledge; an experience gap can also be the driving force. If a keynote speaker or presentation resonates with your journey, if their experiences mirror or inspire your own aspirations, then that connection becomes all the more promising.

And finally, the allure of a business gap. Perhaps the individual leads an organization you dream to be a part of, just like my case with Nelson, or they work for a company aligned with your personal mission statement.

But what if the connection isn't promising?

If the individual doesn't possess the insights you seek, then initiating a networking discussion might only lead to lackluster and time-wasting conversations. We must cherish time as our most valuable asset and avoid spending it on someone who can't support our career growth. Vulnerability is inevitable in networking sessions, so choose wisely - connect with those who can genuinely help you.

In short, make every promising first interaction a stepping stone, while any unpromising encounter should gracefully become the last.

Schedule: Influencer Meetings

Now that we've established a promising connection, the next step is to kick off the "Networking Life Cycle" and schedule a meeting with your influencer. If you're an extrovert like Willie, setting up time on an executive's calendar might come naturally. But for those who find it nerve-wracking, fear not - there are unknown professionals out there who genuinely want to connect with you where you are today. Networking need not be daunting, and you can overcome introversion with small, gradual steps.

To set up time with an influencer, first review your weekly work schedule to assess your flexibility. If your personal time is limited, consider scheduling networking meetings outside work hours - maybe lunch every other Wednesday or coffee chats before work on Fridays. Alternatively, if certain days are less packed with tasks, block time on those days for networking endeavors. For those with fluid schedules, intermingling networking activities within the workday can be an effective approach.

When finding a suitable time to meet, consider the influencer's schedule alongside yours. Unless in a career emergency, it's best to schedule the first meeting 3 to 6 weeks after the initial interaction. Approach this process with confidence, as it sets the stage for your networking journey.

Now, when an influencer has an administrative assistant (admin), it's essential to build a positive relationship with them. The admin serves as the gatekeeper to the influencer's calendar, and a good rapport ensures smoother scheduling. Conversely, a strained relationship could lead to rescheduled or canceled meetings. In the case of an influencer with an admin, email both the executive and the admin when reaching out to set up a meeting. Offer a brief introduction of yourself, share why you'd like to meet, and propose a few suggested dates and times.

However, if an influencer doesn't have an admin, mutually pick an available date and time. In such cases, the onus falls on you to initiate the connection by sending a meeting invitation with a thoughtful message. This approach not only saves time on back-and-forth emails but also shows your genuine interest in meeting them.

To optimize your networking experience, avoid scheduling back-to-back meetings whenever possible. It's crucial to allow a 15-minute gap between networking sessions. This buffer enables you to debrief mentally after one meeting and prepare for the next, ensuring you can be fully present and engaged with each influencer. Back-to-back meetings can be overwhelming, leaving you feeling underprepared and mentally drained.

In instances where unavoidable back-to-back meetings occur, manage your time effectively. Set a 5-minute reminder on your phone for the end of the first meeting, allowing you to conclude respectfully and be on time for the second. Remember, effective time management is key in such scenarios.

In my experience, I schedule meetings with Nelson with a 15-minute buffer before and after. This helps me avoid back-to-back conflicts and ensures a smoother networking experience. By being mindful of scheduling and leaving space for reflection and transition, you'll elevate the quality and impact of your networking conversations.

Career in Action Activity: Schedule your mentor hit list

Now it's time to take action and start scheduling those vital networking meetings. If you've completed the previous assignments, you're well-prepared for this next step.

Begin by setting up just one meeting with one person from your mentor hit list within the next 24 hours. Remember, start small - take that first step with confidence! Reach out to your chosen influencer, introduce yourself, and propose a few available dates and times for the meeting. If they have an admin, include them in the email as well.

Career in Action Activity: Schedule your mentor hit list *(cont)*

But we won't stop there. Challenge yourself to schedule meetings with five more influencers by next week! Embrace this opportunity to connect with professionals who can offer valuable insights and guidance on your career journey.

Remember, your networking success lies in taking consistent action. Don't hesitate; seize the moment to build meaningful connections that can transform your career. Keep the momentum going, and you'll be amazed at the doors that open and the growth that unfolds. So go ahead, schedule those meetings, and watch your network expand before your eyes! Let's make it happen!

Prepare: Pre-Networking

"Luck Favors the Prepared" Edna "E" Mode fictional character in the pixar movie Incredibles

When it comes to networking, preparation is the key to success. After setting up a meeting with an influencer like CMO Mrs. Jazz, it's essential to maximize your time together and ensure a fruitful discussion.

To prepare for the initial "kick-off" meeting, start by doing thorough research on the influencer. Discover potential talking points and common connections that can serve as icebreakers during the conversation. This research will also help you tailor insightful questions and gain credibility with the influencer.

Before my first conversation with Nelson, I did some home-work via Google and LinkedIn. It was helpful to confirm the things he said about his business, learn about other projects he worked on, and gain insight into his family. This research provided me with a clearer picture of the man I was going to meet and helped me create specific questions around transitions in his career.

Another crucial aspect of preparation is having your "hello slide" ready. This slide offers an overview of yourself and guides the conversation, making sure important topics are covered. Creating an early draft of my "hello slide" and seeking feedback from mentors like Nelson greatly improved my networking approach.

Crafting a meeting agenda is equally important. It clarifies the purpose of the discussion and helps you stay on track during the meeting. My first agenda with Nelson was very concise. It included presenting my "Hello Slide", discussing recent successes of Nelson's organization, and asking questions based on the information I researched about him.

Confirming the meeting with the influencer via a quick email before the day saves time and minimizes the frustration of last-minute rescheduling. Networking meetings can be subject to changes, and it's best to be prepared for such situations.

For a meeting with Nelson, I would send an email with the subject: "Timothy Nelson Touch base." The body of the email would read: "Dear Nelson, I'm looking forward to our discussion today. Does 3 pm still work for you? If so, I look forward to our conversation. If not, no worries, I'll look for a time for us to reschedule. Best, Timothy." Once I got a response, I knew the status of our scheduled discussion. If not, I was mentally prepared if the meeting got a last-minute reschedule.

Arriving early for both in-person and virtual meetings is essential for a relaxed and comfortable start. It shows respect for the influencer's time and gives you an opportunity to settle in before diving into the discussion.

To prepare for recurring "follow-up" meetings, refresh your "snapshot slide" with updated information and review your "connection tool," which acts as a digital rolodex for tracking networking details. This step is crucial, especially for distant meetings like the ones I had with Nelson. Reviewing the "connection tool" helped our discussions flow seamlessly, remaining engaging and meaningful.

As you engage in more networking, the preparation process becomes second nature, making your interactions with influencers more productive and rewarding. Remember, the more prepared you are, the luckier you become in forging meaningful connections and advancing your career.

Meet: During Networking

Welcome to the main stage of the networking life cycle: the engaging conversation sparring between you and an influencer - the networking meeting.

You've already come a long way in your networking journey. From that brief encounter with Mrs. Jazz at the conference to scheduling a meeting and preparing your networking tools, now it's time for the real action. Building a superior network for your skyscraper career journey depends on how well you execute the actions in this section.

As my clients take these actions and make them uniquely their own using the Bruce Lee Method, the results are truly career-altering. They end up creating strong connections with powerful people, having consistent, engaging, and meaningful networking discussions. There's a domino effect where the better you get at networking discussions, the more engaging they become, leading to more influencers in your corner. And with more influencers backing you, you have a better chance to exceed your career goals and reach new heights in your career.

In this main stage, we'll break down the mini actions for both types of networking meetings: the kick-off and follow-up meetings. These actions are designed for a typical 30-minute one-on-one conversation with an influencer, which is a standard meeting timing for a networking connection.

Whether you're an expert networker or somewhere in between, the tips and tricks outlined in the actions below will benefit you. No matter what your networking goal is - be it finding a mentor to guide you, getting hired into your dream career by a leader, or having a peer to hold you accountable in tough business decisions - I want to help you achieve it.

So, let's dive in and master the art of networking meetings, ensuring that every conversation is a stepping stone toward your soaring career aspirations.

Strategies for the Initial "Kick Off" meeting

Let's approach the initial "kick off" meeting with finesse and confidence. Start the conversation by giving a quick rundown of the agenda topics. This sets an efficient tone and puts you in control of the discussion before you even begin, creating a smooth flow into your "Hello Slide".

Present your "Hello Slide" just as you practiced with your accountability partner. With practice, this shouldn't take more than a few minutes. Be sure to bring up any stories from the slide that will connect with the influencer, making it engaging and relatable.

After your presentation, show genuine interest in the influencer's career by asking about their journey. Take notes during the conversation, as these will serve as good talking points for future discussions.

If the influencer seems uncomfortable opening up, don't push it. Respect their boundaries and move on to the agenda topics.

Next, remind them why you sought this connection in the first place. Whether it was to learn more about their department, a referral from a mutual connection, or their impressive presentation skills, bring it up as a friendly reminder of your shared interest.

End the conversation with well-prepared questions. A well-phrased question can lead to an engaging dialogue, and you might find it hard to get the influencer to stop talking!

Don't forget to ask for a follow-up conversation at the end of the "kick-off" discussion. This shows your interest in building a deeper relationship and keeps the networking cycle going. Set up a recurring series of meetings to maintain regular contact.

Remember, these meetings are not interviews. Have fun and enjoy the discussion. Smile, add humor where appropriate, and be yourself. If the conversation goes off course, don't worry. You can always follow up with networking documentation and questions afterward.

In my "kick-off" meeting with Nelson, we already had a great rapport from a golf event. I knew what to cover and had burning questions ready. We chatted about his family briefly, but he was focused on helping me and gave valuable insights on my "Hello Slide" and his own business journey. We agreed to meet every six months for 30 minutes, a decision that has strengthened our relationship.

Approach your networking meetings with confidence and authenticity, and you'll create meaningful connections that can shape your career in powerful ways.

Strategies For the Recurring "Follow-Up" meeting

Congratulations on successfully landing a recurring meeting with an influencer! This is where the networking life cycle repeats, and you have a chance to strengthen your connection even further. As I experienced with Nelson, each recurring meeting allowed us to learn more about each other's lives, creating a stronger bond both personally and professionally.

Open your "follow-up" meeting just like you did in the "kick-off" conversation, covering the agenda topics and reminding them of the networking goal. This gentle reminder reinforces the importance of the meeting.

Start with some personal questions to ease into the discussion. Inquire about their family, pets, recent trips, or other personal matters you've noted about them. Building rapport through these soft personal references sets the stage for a more engaging and fruitful conversation.

Next, transition into work discussions, perhaps by asking about their current workload or diving into your "snapshot slide." Observe their reactions and cues to identify the topics that interest them the most. Let the conversation flow naturally, and be prepared to delve deeper into any points that catch their attention.

Share your "snapshot slide" and use it as a tool for an interactive tennis match discussion. Stop at each bullet point and explore further when the influencer shows interest. Allow the conversation to follow the influencer's lead, discussing items that intrigue them.

Towards the end, seek advice or ask questions related to your short-term goals. Showing attentiveness to their perspective is vital in creating a strong connection.

And don't forget to highlight any recent work successes, even if you have only a minute left. Mention your biggest win to date, whether it's a successful project, cost-saving initiative, or new program you started. This showcases your ability to execute, making you a potential candidate for future roles.

Over the years, as I met with Nelson multiple times, our connection deepened. Our conversations evolved from discussing weekend activities to delving into more significant issues like social justice. On the professional front, we went from project updates to strategizing on managing difficult conversations with managers.

By following these strategies, you can nurture your networking relationships into strong, meaningful connections that will support your career growth and lead you to success. Remember, building genuine relationships takes time and effort, but the rewards are worth it in the long run. Keep engaging with influencers and honing your networking skills for a bright and prosperous career journey.

Debrief: Post-Networking

To successfully execute *the skyscraper method*, there are three crucial actions you must take after every networking meeting: sending a thank you email, updating the "connection tool," and following up on any action items discussed during the meeting.

Just like you would after an interview, it's essential to send a thank you email to the influencer within 48 hours of the networking meeting. Express your gratitude for their time and include some discussion points or takeaways from your conversation. Don't hesitate to add a touch of humor if the conversation was light-hearted. Tailor the email to make it more personable and specific to your discussion.

Below is an example of a thank you email I sent to a mentor on my hit list. This one is very general, make your version more personable and specific to your conversation (Bruce Lee Method).

Subject Line: Thank You

Dear *[Mr./Ms. Last Name]*:

Thank you very much for the opportunity to chat yesterday *[or today, if appropriate]*. I appreciate your candor and openness to discuss your background and your organization *[or, if follow-up meeting, a personal or professional update discussed]*. I am very interested in continuing our discussion about *[knowledge gap]*.

[For, Kick Off Meetings] I'll look for time to schedule our next discussion. As per our conversation, I'd love to set up a recurring meeting *[with your admin, if appropriate]* every 3 months *[or more, if appropriate]*. I'll take your advice and *[suggested influencer advice]*.

Before our next call, I plan on *[1 action takeaway here]*.

Attached is my "Hello Slide" *[or "Snapshot Slide," if appropriate]* shared in our discussion.

Again, thank you for the time. Look forward to our next touch base.

Best Regards,
[Your Name]

Once the email is sent, open your "connection tool" and jot down notes about the conversation. These notes will prove invaluable for any follow-up discussions and help you keep track of important details.

Lastly, act on any suggested tasks or action items discussed during the networking meeting. This could include specific tasks related to work assignments, following up with leaders, or researching recommended resources. By completing these follow-up items, you demonstrate credibility and commitment to the influencer.

In my recurring meetings with Nelson, I always acted on his small suggestions, which led to better performance reviews from my manager and eventually a promotion. Sharing the results of these actions during our subsequent meetings added even more impact and value to our conversations.

By following these post-networking strategies, you set yourself apart from others, show your dedication to staying connected, and build stronger relationships with influencers. Debriefing after each networking meeting will help you assess whether it was successful or not.

Successful Meeting vs. Unsuccessful Meeting

After each networking meeting, it's crucial to evaluate its success before moving on to the next step in the networking life cycle. I always ask myself one question: "Was the meeting successful?" A successful meeting is characterized by meaningful topics of discussion that benefit both myself and the influencer. The conversation flows naturally with a back-and-forth exchange of fresh perspectives. On the other hand, an unsuccessful meeting feels forced, the influencer seems awkward, and no new insights are gained.

Quality over quantity is my approach to networking. I prioritize building relationships with leaders where meetings are fruitful, and we both experience personal and professional growth. This self-check process helps me nurture the best connections and let go of those that don't serve me well.

In my networking journey, I've found that successful meetings are more common, but there are instances when an unsuccessful meeting occurs. To help you assess your own networking interactions, let's look at some hypothetical situations involving our characters, Willie Smyth and Mrs. Jazz. I'll grade these scenarios like a teacher, on an A through F scale, and provide a recommended next step. Enjoy the scenarios!

Grade	Scenario	Recommended Next Step
F	Scenario 1: During the meeting with Mrs. Jazz, Willie faced multiple signs of disinterest. Mrs. Jazz didn't engage in the conversation, checked her watch repeatedly, avoided eye contact, and left awkward silences. In retrospect, Willie felt that Mrs. Jazz wasn't enthusiastic about the meeting. Scenario 2: After the initial kickoff meeting, Mrs. Jazz declines all follow-up requests and ignores Willie's emails. When they meet again at a conference, she acts as if they have never met.	It's evident that Mrs. Jazz is not interested in maintaining a networking relationship with Willie. In such cases, it's best for Willie to discontinue pursuing further connections with her. It's essential to recognize when a networking relationship isn't mutually beneficial and move on to build more meaningful connections with other influencers

C	Scenario 1: During the meeting, Mrs. Jazz went off-topic, talking extensively about her breakfast selection for 20 minutes, which had nothing to do with the intended agenda. Scenario 2: The meeting with Mrs. Jazz ended 15 minutes early as she rushed through the conversation, providing brief responses and constantly asking, "Ok. What's next?" after every statement from Willie. Scenario 3: Willie felt drained during the conversation because he had to repeat questions to get any interaction from Mrs. Jazz. He's now contemplating whether to continue the meeting series.	These networking scenarios could be isolated incidents, and the next meeting might turn out to be amazing. Willie should apply the Bruce Lee Method and honestly assess if these situations are random occurrences or consistent patterns of behavior from the influencer. If it's a recurring pattern, he should seriously consider ending the professional relationship to focus on more productive connections.
B	Scenario 1: During the meeting, Mrs. Jazz actively engaged with Willie's presentation and asked insightful questions. They had a detailed discussion about Willie's next career move, and Mrs. Jazz provided actionable advice for his short-term goals. They successfully covered all agenda items, and after the meeting, Mrs. Jazz responded to Willie's thank you email with an equally appreciative response. Scenario 2: Mrs. Jazz went above and beyond by providing Willie with contact information from	With all these positive signs, it's clear that Willie should absolutely continue nurturing this networking relationship. The engagement and mutual value displayed during the meeting are strong indicators of a fruitful and beneficial connection. Networking is all about building meaningful relationships, and it seems like Willie has found a valuable ally in Mrs. Jazz

	her network to help him achieve a specific goal. Scenario 3: The meeting was so engaging and fruitful that they both lost track of time, ending up 15 minutes over the scheduled meeting end time. Both Mrs. Jazz and Willie enjoyed the conversation so much that they didn't want it to end.	who can contribute significantly to his professional growth and success.
A	Scenario 1: During the meeting, Mrs. Jazz is so impressed with Willie's core skills showcased on his "Snapshot Slide" that she extends a verbal job offer right there. Recognizing the value and potential Willie brings, Mrs. Jazz is eager to have him as part of her team. This kind of immediate job offer is a clear indication of a highly successful networking meeting. Scenario 2: The relationship between Willie and Mrs. Jazz extends beyond the professional realm. Mrs. Jazz values Willie not only as a potential colleague but also as a friend. She invites Willie to attend a personal function, such as a family-friendly event, demonstrating a genuine interest in getting to know him on a more personal level.	Without a doubt, these scenarios indicate a highly successful networking connection. In both cases, the networking cycle resets, and Willie and Mrs. Jazz are well on their way to building a strong and mutually beneficial relationship. This is what networking is all about—forging authentic relationships that lead to exciting opportunities and lasting friendships.

Making the decision to discontinue a networking relationship isn't always straightforward. While you can use the grading scale for some guidance, ultimately, your intuition will play a significant role in determining if the conversation was successful or not. As you strive to become a superior networker, I recommend focusing on maintaining only those professional relationships that have proven to be successful and meaningful.

How to resume the networking life cycle?

Now, let's talk about how to resume the networking life cycle after a successful meeting. It's a simple process—schedule another meeting with the same influencer. There are two ways to do this. The first approach involves referring back to the steps described earlier in the scheduling stage and manually setting up a meeting. However, the challenge with this method is that it's easy to forget to schedule a networking meeting amidst our busy lives.

The second and most effective way to restart the "networking life cycle" is by setting up a recurring meeting with the influencer. This feature is often underutilized in calendar applications, but it's a game-changer. For instance, you can schedule a meeting for the last Thursday of every 3 months for the next 5 years. This way, you ensure regular engagements and build a deeper and more consistent connection. Plus, if any scheduling conflicts arise, you can easily adjust the meeting well in advance, and most influencers are accommodating to such changes.

So, take advantage of recurring meetings to maintain a steady and meaningful networking cadence. It keeps you on track to build strong relationships with influencers and reap the rewards of a well-nurtured network. With this approach, you'll be well-prepared to seize opportunities and accelerate your career growth.

The Last Interaction:

How to gracefully discontinue a professional relationship?

The process is straightforward. Start by communicating with your influencer that you'll be canceling any follow-up meetings and then proceed to cancel those meetings. Here's a sample email below:

Subject Line: Thank You

Dear *Mr./Ms. Last Name:*

Thank you very much for the opportunity to meet. I appreciate your candor and openness to discuss your background and your organization *[or, if follow-up meeting, a personal or professional update discussed]*.

Attached is my "Hello Slide" *[or "Snapshot Slide," if appropriate]* shared in our discussion.
[For discontinuing a follow- up meeting: I currently have competing obligations and I'll make sure to reach out to you for future discussions when time permits.]
[For discontinuing a kick off: Again, thank you for the time.]

Best Regards,
Your Name

Once the email is sent, proceed to cancel any follow-up meetings with that influencer. This professional approach will bring closure to our networking relationship and make our previous meeting the last interaction.

In my earlier years of consistent networking, I often found myself meeting with leaders who earned F or even C grades in our interactions. My logic was quantity over quality, thinking that the more people I knew, the greater my chances of advancing in my career. However, looking back, I realized I spent hours preparing and meeting with individuals who didn't contribute to my growth. I regret not ending those networking relationships sooner.

I share this because I want you to avoid falling into the same trap. Use your time wisely and apply the *skyscraper method* to network efficiently only with influencers who genuinely want to engage with you. This might mean resetting your current network by ending unfulfilling relationships and starting fresh with influencers who will truly help you progress in your desired direction. Remember, it's not about the quantity of connections, but the quality of those relationships that will propel your career forward.

In this chapter, we have delved into the essential building blocks of constructing your career skyscraper through the art of networking. By embracing the "networking life cycle", you have equipped yourself with the tools and strategies to initiate successful connections with influencers. From crafting your "Hello Slide" to preparing for kick-off meetings and follow-ups, you have honed the skills necessary to make meaningful and productive interactions.

Throughout the process, we have explored various scenarios and graded the outcomes to help you discern the effectiveness of your networking efforts. Whether it's an A-grade encounter with an influencer who extends a job offer based on your core skills or a C-grade meeting that leaves you uncertain about the future, these experiences have taught you valuable lessons about building a robust and influential professional network.

Now, as the building phase comes to a close, it's time to transition into the next phase: servicing. This phase is all about networking hacks - the top tricks to elevate your networking game to the next level. Here, we will explore innovative strategies to maximize the benefits of your networking connections, fine-tune your approach for even greater success, and overcome challenges that may arise in your networking journey.

With the foundation of your career skyscraper firmly established, you are now prepared for more advanced techniques that will take your networking skills from good to exceptional. The servicing phase will empower you to streamline your networking process, efficiently manage your connections, and cultivate stronger, more lasting relationships with influencers. Through these hacks, you'll gain access to exclusive opportunities, accelerate your career growth, and position yourself as a respected and influential figure in your industry.

Let's embark on this exciting phase together and make your career dreams a reality. Onward to networking greatness!

▶ Phase 6: Servicing

Skyscraper Method

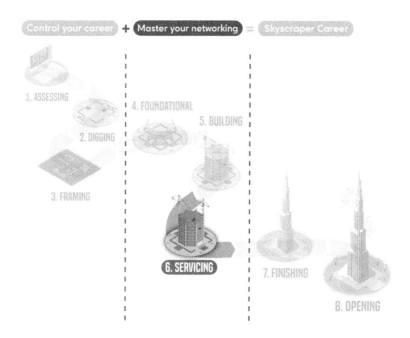

In the grand process of building a skyscraper, after the construction phase, lies a critical juncture known as the "Servicing" phase. This phase is of utmost importance as it sets the stage for the longevity and stability of the towering structure. It involves completing the finishing touches, ensuring all components are functioning seamlessly, and securing the foundation for the skyscraper to withstand the tests of time and weather the storms that may come its way.

Similarly, in your career journey, the Servicing phase marks a pivotal moment. It's the phase where you've already laid the groundwork by acquiring the necessary skills and experiences during the Building phase. Now, it's time to focus on deepening your foundations and elevating your connections to reach greater heights in your professional life.

Networking during the Servicing phase becomes paramount. Connecting with executive leaders and influential professionals can open doors to opportunities that might have remained elusive otherwise. Mastering networking during this phase will be instrumental in propelling you towards your career goals, making the process of constructing your skyscraper journey more manageable and successful.

As you progress through this chapter, you'll discover three essential networking hacks that will help you become a superior networker and master the art of deepening relationships with executive leaders.

Hack 1: Use Pocket Blockers:

Just as the Servicing phase involves placing certain elements of the skyscraper on hold until the right time, the "Pocket Blockers" networking hack allows you to strategically place an open job opportunity on hold until the timing is perfect. This technique enables you to nurture your relationships with executive leaders, gain their insights, and position yourself as the ideal candidate when the time is ripe for that coveted position.

Hack 2: Kill Procrastination:

A skyscraper's core is essential for its stability, and similarly, overcoming procrastination is fundamental to your networking success. In this section, we'll share invaluable tips to conquer procrastination, stay focused on your networking goals, and build the inner strength needed to forge enduring connections with executive leaders.

Hack 3: Share Annual Newsletters:

A skyscraper's supporting pillars bear the weight of the entire structure, just as your network's influencers provide support and guidance in your career journey. The networking hack of sending an annual newsletter to influencers allows you to maintain and deepen multiple networking relationships simultaneously. By providing valuable updates on your progress, you solidify your position in their minds and foster lasting connections.

Each of these networking hacks serves as a crucial tool in the Servicing phase of your career development. When applied effectively, they will undoubtedly enhance your networking abilities and position you as a superior networker, capable of navigating the landscape of executive leadership connections with ease.

In the following chapters, we'll delve into the specifics of each networking hack. We'll equip you with the necessary strategies and techniques to master each one, allowing you to strengthen the foundation of your skyscraper journey and elevate your career prospects.

So, as you embark on this phase of deepening connections and fostering meaningful relationships, remember that networking is not about instant gratification but rather about investing in a sustainable and thriving network that will serve you for years to come. By understanding and embracing the significance of the Servicing phase, you are setting yourself up for a rewarding and successful career ascent.

With these networking hacks in your toolkit, you're ready to embark on a journey towards becoming a superior networker. Let's dive into each hack and unleash the true potential of your networking prowess in the chapters that follow.

Chapter 13:
Use Networking Hacks

Welcome to the ultimate guide on taking your networking game to a whole new level! In this section, I'm about to unleash three powerful strategies that I like to call "Networking Hacks" designed to make networking using *the skyscraper method* an attainable reality for you. So, keep on your hard hat because we're about to elevate your connections and scale new heights together.

As previously stated the 3 hacks are: Use "Pocket Blockers", Kill Procrastination, and Share Annual Highlights.

By now, you might be wondering, "How will these hacks make my skyscraper journey more manageable?" Well, it's simple - these networking hacks will empower you to harness the potential of your network, maximize your connections, and build a tower of opportunities that seemed unattainable before.

So, get ready to level up your networking skills, supercharge your career journey, and unlock a world of possibilities that lie beyond the horizon. In this chapter, we'll explain each hack, equip you with insider tips, and set you on a course to become a true networking ninja.

Hack 1: "Pocket Blockers" - Mastering the Art of Selective Pursuit

As we've discussed in earlier chapters, networking is a powerful tool that builds credibility with influencers, leading to fruitful discussions about potential job opportunities. However, what happens when an influencer presents you with a job offer that you're not quite ready for or doesn't align with your long-term career goals? Enter the "pocket blocker" strategy - a skillful move inspired by my love for games like spades, bowling, and pool.

Imagine you're playing a game of pool, and one of your balls ends up right at the edge of a pocket. This situation can be compared to a job opportunity presented to you by an influential figure. Now, you face a crucial decision: do you impulsively knock the ball into the pocket and make a quick move, or do you strategically block the pocket for later use?

In the world of career development, this choice can be challenging. Let's take a fictional scenario involving Willie Smyth and his executive mentor, Mrs. Jazz. Mrs. Jazz excitedly offers Willie a role on her team, believing he'd be an ideal candidate. While the opportunity seems tempting, Willie is torn because his current job aligns perfectly with his long-term career goals.

In this situation, Willie has three options: he can swiftly accept the new job, decline it immediately, or, like a seasoned pool player, employ the "pocket blocker" strategy. The third option involves expressing interest in the opportunity, learning more about it, and communicating the possibility of pursuing it when the time is right. Just like the pool player who strategically leaves the ball by the pocket to limit the opponent's options, Willie can maintain his strong relationship with Mrs. Jazz while being deliberate about his career choices.

By employing the "pocket blocker" strategy, you can gracefully navigate these scenarios without jeopardizing valuable relationships or making impulsive decisions. Remember, networking is not just about jumping at every opportunity; it's about strategic timing and making decisions that align with your long-term career goals.

How to execute the "Pocket Blocker" strategy - A Tactical Approach to Superior Networking

In the "pocket blocker" scenario, Willie Smyth displays the finesse of a master networker by deftly handling a job opportunity presented to him by his executive mentor, Mrs. Jazz. Here's how Willie executes the "pocket blocker" strategy to perfection:

Step 1: Show Genuine Interest and Seek Information Willie begins by expressing sincere appreciation to Mrs. Jazz for considering him as an asset to her team. He artfully engages her by saying, "I would love to learn more. Tell me about the role and its responsibilities. What's your vision for this position?" By showing keen interest, he deepens their networking relationship, demonstrating to Mrs. Jazz that she can entrust him with her ideas and count on him as a valuable ally.

Step 2: Connect with Recommended Contacts The next move in the pocket blocker playbook is to reach out to the contacts Mrs. Jazz recommended. Willie sets up 30-minute informational conversations with each one. During these discussions, he skillfully introduces himself using his "hello slide" and then delves into questions about the open job opportunity. He inquires about what led to the role being vacant, the challenges involved, and the path to success for someone in that position. This approach provides Willie with valuable insights, allowing him to make informed decisions.

Step 3: Communicate Wisely with Mrs. Jazz having gathered ample information, Willie circles back to Mrs. Jazz and communicates the key discussion points from his conversations with her contacts. He highlights anything promising about the job but closes by gracefully expressing that he won't be pursuing the opportunity at this time. By conducting thorough due diligence, Willie demonstrates his seriousness about making the right moves at the right time. Mrs. Jazz respects his decision, keeps him top of mind for future opportunities, and sustains their networking life cycle.

The Power of "Pocket Blocking" - A Win-Win Strategy

The 'pocket blocker' strategy is a masterstroke for several reasons. Firstly, it keeps your influencers engaged in the networking process. Secondly, it prevents you from hastily accepting a job offer that doesn't align with your long-term career journey. Moreover, if the discussions with the recommended contacts yield fruitful results, you can add their names to your "mentor hit list." These connections could prove to be invaluable in the future, should you need to explore new career options urgently.

Willie's experience showcases the effectiveness of pocket blocking. By handling the opportunity with finesse, he maintains his value in the eyes of Mrs. Jazz and positions himself for future prospects. Numerous clients have utilized this savvy strategy, circling back to open roles months later and stepping into those positions with ease when the time is right.

So, as you venture forth in your networking journey, remember the wisdom of pocket blocking. It's not about closing doors but rather about strategically choosing the right ones and confidently navigating your path to success. Keep honing your networking skills, and in the next section, we'll uncover even more networking hacks that will elevate your connections and take your career journey to exhilarating heights.

Hack 2: Kill Procrastination - Get Sh*t Done

Picture yourself facing a critical project with tight deadlines, and you know that every second counts. Yet, instead of diving in and making progress, you find yourself getting lost in the never-ending abyss of social media or engaging in office banter that adds no value to your work. Before you know it, valuable hours have slipped away, and the pressure mounts as the deadline looms. Procrastination in the workplace can lead to missed opportunities, decreased productivity, and needless stress, hindering your career growth.

The *skyscraper method* is a powerful tool for career development, but procrastination can be the difference between success and stagnation. Many clients recognize the potential of this method to catapult them into their dream careers, yet they struggle with finding the time to apply it consistently. They put off essential career-building activities with the thought, "I'll get to it when I can," only to find themselves stuck in a loop of inaction.

To conquer procrastination, remember the wisdom of Desmond Tutu's quote, "When eating an elephant, take one bite at a time." This sage advice was applied when tackling the seemingly impossible task of constructing the Dubai skyscraper, Burj Khalifa, which stands as the world's tallest building. Bit by bit, the impossible was achieved.

Applying the "one bite at a time" strategy to the *skyscraper method* is the key to defeating procrastination. Break down your career development tasks into manageable chunks and plan ahead to tackle them. Schedule specific "project" times in your calendar to work on tasks like crafting your personal mission statement. When the time comes, dive in and make progress, regardless of how much you accomplish in that session. The key is to keep moving forward, taking bites out of the elephant.

To completely slay procrastination, you must also protect your "project" time from distractions. Avoid the siren call of social media, office gossip, or other time-wasting activities. Create a focused environment that allows you to immerse yourself in the task at hand, maximizing productivity.

By mastering the art of time management, planning ahead, and eliminating distractions, you'll effectively quash procrastination and make steady progress on your skyscraper career journey. Remember, success is built upon consistent action, and every step counts toward reaching the pinnacle of your career aspirations.

A. Planning Ahead - One Half of the Procrastination-Slaying

When it comes to killing procrastination, the first half of the hack is all about planning ahead. I've witnessed the transformative power of this strategy firsthand, thanks to a valuable lesson I learned from the esteemed book "*7 Habits of Highly Effective People: Powerful Lessons in Personal Change*" by Steven Covey.

Covey astutely points out that the ideal work environment for accomplishing tasks is when they are important but not yet urgent. And the key to creating this ideal setting lies in proactive planning. He taught me to harness time to create more time - a concept that has been a game-changer for my productivity.

To put this into action, allocate just one hour per week to meticulously schedule the next seven days. If you find yourself short on time, don't fret; start with an hour of planning on a leisurely day like Sunday to set the stage for a productive week ahead. During this planning session, line up all your tasks - be it work-related, personal, or recreational. Carve out specific blocks of time for work, workouts, being a career coach, spending time with family, going on dates, or simply unwinding and doing nothing.

If you come across schedule conflicts, address them head-on by moving or eliminating non-essential items. This way, when the actual week arrives, you'll have a clear roadmap to tackle your high-priority tasks with ease.

Furthermore, strategically plan to complete your most critical tasks when your mind is freshest and sharpest. For me, that's earlier in the day. By knocking out the tougher tasks first, you set the tone for a day of accomplishments and momentum, making the rest of the day flow more effortlessly.

Weekly planning not only sets you up for success but also creates open space for handling urgent and important tasks that might arise unexpectedly, such as family emergencies or work fire drills.

Now, let's apply Covey's wisdom to *the skyscraper method.* Incorporating weekly planning into your routine enables you to prepare for networking meetings, block travel time for influential encounters, and manage your career journey seamlessly. For instance, if you need to update your "snapshot slide" before meeting an influencer, schedule 30 minutes the day before to ensure it gets done. Additionally, set aside time after networking meetings to debrief and update your "connection tool." By planning ahead, you eliminate the need to add these tasks to your to-do list or hope you remember to complete them.

With this proactive approach, you're not only well-prepared to get things done but also shielded from interruptions that could knock you off your career journey.

B. Avoiding Distractions - The Second Half of the Procrastination-Slaying Hack

In our quest to kill procrastination, the second half of the hack centers around taming distractions. Distractions come in various forms, and while some may be beyond our control, there are plenty we can rein in to stay focused on mastering the *Skyscraper Method.* Let's dive into the activities and environments that you have the power to control, ensuring they don't divert you from managing your career journey.

Controllable distractions encompass tasks that are neither important nor urgent. Take, for example, the allure of endless social media scrolling. How often have you found yourself absorbed in information that adds little value to your daily tasks and lacks any sense of urgency?

Then there are those time-sucking activities like video stream-ing, news feeds, web browsing, and the temptation of new TV series. These diversions often lurk on our mobile devices, enticing us into a black hole of time-wasting. For my fellow procrastinators, it might be time to stash away that device designed to keep you engaged for hours on end. Consider physically placing your phone outside of your workspace or putting it in airplane mode. This simple action has proven to be a game-changer, empowering both me and my clients to accomplish more.

Environmental distractions are equally vital to address. The ideal work environment varies from person to person. For instance, I thrive in the tranquility of a quiet library, far away from the beckoning of my phone. On the other hand, my wife thrives in a collaborative, musical workspace, where she can engage with others and discuss mutual challenges. It's essential to identify the work environment that fosters your productiv-ity. Embrace your unique "Bruce Lee Mentality" and harness it to conquer distractions.

As a coach, I integrate this powerful hack into the phases, ensuring my clients plan ahead and schedule their Career in Action Activities. I firmly believe that a desired career is within reach through consistent small steps, dedicated time commitment, and diligent effort.

By mastering the art of planning ahead and avoiding distractions, you're setting yourself up for success in the skyscraper journey of your career. Embrace the discipline to stay focused, and remember each small step you take serves as a stepping stone towards the skyscraper of your dreams!

Hack 3: Share Annual Highlights - Multiply your Networking Impact

Allow me to share a short, impactful story that inspired this final networking hack. It all began on a cold November day when I found myself in a networking meeting with Mrs. Sanders, a supplier diversity executive with a busy schedule and a plethora of responsibilities. As we sat in her plush office, I couldn't help but notice a stack of 30 small green boxes scattered across her desk. Intrigued, I inquired about them before delving into my "snapshot slide". Mrs. Sanders revealed that every year, she sends a note of her accomplishments to her top career supporters, along with a thoughtful Christmas ornament. This act of generosity stunned me, considering her demanding position. However, as we talked more, she enlightened me about the significance of sharing annual highlights with top influencers. It turns out, this was her secret to sustaining crucial connections over time. I learned that this simple gesture of gratitude, accomplishment, sharing, and staying in touch is the key to standing out and maintaining strong relationships.

Inspired by Mrs. Sanders, I followed suit and began sending out my own season's greetings and annual highlight reel to my top influencers. I crafted a holiday email with a PDF of my yearly accomplishments, which held a similar impact to her heartfelt note with an ornament. You can customize your approach, whether it's via email, snail mail, or any other means that resonate with your personal style.

Like Mrs. Sanders and me, our illustrative character, Willie Smyth, will show you how to create and share your annual highlights. Let's say Willie has been diligently executing the *skyscraper method* all year, effectively networking with influencers using his "snapshot slide". In December, he decided to send his top influencers an email showcasing his personal and professional achievements from the year. To compile his highlight reel, he'll document three critical elements: his successes from the current year, his goals for the year to come, and a professional family photo. This well-rounded package will provide his top influencers with a glimpse of his journey thus far and where he's heading.

Willie draws on the larger impact items from his past snapshot slides to compose his highlights. For example, purchasing his first home was a significant personal milestone, and creating a virtual marketing tool that benefits over 200 employees became a proud professional accomplishment. These highlights, among others, culminate in a concise and impressive year-end summary.

Next, Willie pens down the goals he's set for the upcoming year. His list comprises both short-term objectives from his most recent "snapshot slide" and long-term aspirations that he's yet to share. For instance, he mentions his desire to gain a leadership role at his company in his "snapshot slide." In addition, he includes his goal to invest in rental property in Los Angeles, a target for the forthcoming year.

Lastly, to add a personal touch, Willie arranges a professional family photoshoot to obtain a recent family photo.

Once he has all the elements ready, Willie compiles a one-page holiday newsletter, elegantly presenting his highlights and goals. To ensure the document remains intact, he converts it into a non-editable PDF format. He then crafts a warm, personalized holiday email for his top ten influencers. In the email, he expresses his gratitude for their support, references his "connection tool" for something personal shared during their interactions, and invites them to view his attached annual highlights.

Here's an example of both the PDF and Email:

Dear Alex,

Season's Greetings! I wanted to extend my heartfelt thanks for your invaluable advice this year. Your words have directly contributed to my career growth. I'm thrilled about the success of your new technology business; you're poised to revolutionize the sales industry. I hope your family enjoys the upcoming holiday trip to Aspen this winter. Attached are my annual highlights. I look forward to reconnecting in the new year.

Best regards,

Willie

SAMPLE *Happy Holidays*

Personal Highlights
- ✓ Purchased new home in Charlotte, North Carolina
- ✓ Led the Virtual Book Club, with ~50 members
  - ○ Completed **12** books covering topics on improving financial acumen, thinking effectively, measuring happiness, and becoming a successful leader
- ✓ Started a charity organization to raise monetary donations, canned goods, and school supplies for various organizations based in the Charlotte community.

Professional Highlights
- ✓ Completed the development of an Interactive Marketing tool, a communication request aggregator, which interacts with over 200 associates.
- ✓ Developed a you tube advertisement framework, to market technology benefits to young adults. Once approved, ads to be released 2025
- ✓ Mentored 13 summer interns

2025
I plan on building a foundation for leadership opportunities!

Personal Goals
- ✓ Raise over $5,000 in monetary donations, canned goods, clothing, toiletries, and school supplies for charity
- ✓ Complete 12 books that will expand my mind, teach me new skills, and sharpen my current skills
- ✓ Purchase 2 rental properties in Los Angeles

Professional Goals
- ✓ Gain leadership opportunities within the company on marketing projects that high visibility
- ✓ Develop a groundbreaking process improvement for the Branding team
- ✓ Become an active member of an Employee Network outside of my sphere of influence

Again, Happy Holidays and Thank You!!!

Willie Smyth

To add an extra dash of intrigue and ensure his email stands out, Willie sends it at an odd time - 10 AM on a Sunday. This clever strategy ensures that the email hits the inbox of his influencers when there's little to no email traffic, thus capturing their undivided attention.

This end-to-end process for Willie usually takes around 35 minutes to complete. Ever since that enlightening encounter with Mrs. Sanders and her green boxes, I've been diligently sending annual highlight emails. The results of this extra networking activity have been nothing short of exponential. I've received return emails filled with gratitude, invitations to holiday events, thoughtful gifts, and even job offers for some of my clients! The key lies in staying top of mind, relevant, and connected with your top influencers. By sharing your annual highlights, you'll fortify your connections and take your career journey to soaring heights.

Congratulations! You've successfully navigated through the "Servicing" phase, where we explored three powerful networking hacks that will undoubtedly deepen your relationships with executive leaders and propel your career to extraordinary heights. With the art of pocket blockers, you've learned to be strategic and patient, making sure you're always ready for the right opportunity that aligns with your long-term career goals. By conquering procrastination through planning ahead and avoiding distractions, you've unlocked the ability to stay focused and productive, conquering tasks with ease. Lastly, sharing your annual highlights with top influencers has become your secret weapon, fostering a sense of gratitude and connection that keeps you top of mind and relevant in the minds of those who matter most.

As you've embraced these networking hacks, you've ignited sparks that add a touch of brilliance to your skyscraper journey - a career of endless possibilities and accomplishments. But the journey doesn't end here. In fact, we are about to close out the *skyscraper method* with strength and determination. Our grand finale awaits!

Now, it's time to move on to the "Finishing" phase, where we'll cover the importance of becoming an avid reader and a person who gives back. These two essential components will be the pillars that elevate your career. Being an avid reader will open the doors to boundless knowledge, insights, and fresh perspectives that will inspire and guide your every step. Learning from the successes and experiences of others will provide you with the wisdom and strategies to navigate the complex world of career development with ease.

Additionally, embracing the art of giving back will not only enrich your life but also elevate your standing in the professional world. As you lend a helping hand, share your expertise, and give back to your community and industry, you'll become a valued and respected figure among your peers and executives alike. Your generosity will be the cornerstone of lasting connections and a network that continues to grow and support you throughout your career journey.

So, my fellow skyscraper builders, as we prepare to venture into the "Finishing" phase, remember the three invaluable networking hacks you've mastered during the "Servicing" phase. Keep your pocket blockers at the ready, tackle procrastination with careful planning, and share your annual highlights with a heart full of gratitude. You're primed to achieve new heights in your career.

Now, let's embark on this final leg of our journey, ready to embrace the magic of reading and the joy of giving. The "Finishing" phase awaits!

▶ Phase 7: Finishing

Skyscraper Method

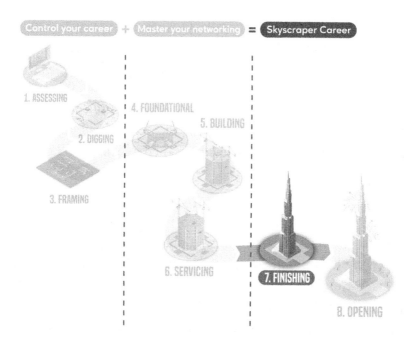

In the previous chapters, we've covered the entire *skyscraper method*, from its initial assessment stage to the crucial servicing phase. Now, as we delve into the "Finishing" phase, we find ourselves ready to put the final touches on our metaphorical skyscraper. This phase is all about reinforcing the *skyscraper method* by incorporating two essential techniques: the thirst for knowledge and giving back to others.

Just like the final stages of constructing a physical skyscraper, the "Finishing" phase is vital for the completion and refinement of our career journey. It is here that we solidify the foundation laid in the previous phases, bringing the entire method to fruition. By embracing the techniques of thirst for knowledge and giving back, we ensure its longevity.

Technique 1: Thirst for Knowledge

In this phase, I urge you to become an avid reader, continuously seeking new information and insights. Like adding floors and choosing furniture within a completed skyscraper, this thirst for knowledge enhances and beautifies our career journey. As you become proficient in gathering knowledge from diverse sources, your ideas become more sophisticated, and your networking conversations become more intellectually Stimulating.

Technique 2: Giving Back

As we continue the "Finishing" phase, we add the element of giving back to others. This phase corresponds to the act of philanthropy and community involvement in the construction process of a skyscraper. Giving back completes a sense of purpose within your personal mission statement and provides a higher level of fulfillment in your career journey.

The act of giving back is twofold: it benefits both your community and your own career. Volunteering and supporting others not only create a positive impact on those you help but also evoke a profound sense of gratitude within yourself. This appreciation reinforces your career goals, giving them a deeper meaning and motivation.

As your career skyscraper grows stronger and taller, it becomes more resilient to potential pitfalls. The thirst for knowledge arms you with the wisdom to navigate complexities, while giving back nurtures a network that will stand by you during difficult times. The symbiotic relationship between these techniques ensures the sustainability of your career tower for the long term.

Embracing the "Finishing" phase techniques and applying them as needed reflects the Bruce Lee Mentality of adaptability and continuous improvement.

As we transition into the next chapter, we'll focus on the transformative power of becoming an avid reader. We will explore the art of reading and how it complements the *skyscraper method*, enabling you to scale new heights in your career journey.

In summary, the "Finishing" phase is the crowning glory of the *skyscraper method*. By embracing the techniques of thirst for knowledge and giving back, you fortify your career tower, ensuring its resilience, and shaping it to touch the skies.

Chapter 14:
Thirst for Knowledge

"Open a Book, Open your Mind." - Charles Chiltington, fictional character from the novel Escape from Mr. Lemoncello's Library

How many books have you truly delved into over the past year? Have any of those books inspired you to make meaningful changes in your life? Let me tell you, cultivating a habit of reading isn't just an occasional pastime; it's a lifestyle that can revolutionize your journey through the *skyscraper method*. Just as a skyscraper's strength is built from the ground up, your career tower gains newfound resilience and ascendancy through the power of reading.

Not an avid reader? I can relate. I've transformed from an occasional reader, who could barely manage a book every couple of years, into a voracious devourer of knowledge, absorbing around 30 books annually. It all began with a single talk, a public speaker who passionately expounded on the transformative potential of reading. His words struck a chord, igniting the spark that set ablaze my unquenchable thirst for knowledge.

Since then, I've experienced seismic shifts in my life due to the books I've read. I've acquired diverse skills – from honing the art of persuasion to mastering the kitchen, from understanding the intricacies of financial markets to deciphering negotiation tactics. Moreover, I've been privy to the insights of the world's greatest minds – hearing tales from Navy seals, gleaning strategies from corporate titans, and embracing wisdom from millionaire entrepreneurs. It's astonishing how the pages of a book can reshape your perspective, infuse you with practical skills, and embolden your ambitions.

But what does reading really do for your career, you ask? It fortifies your cognitive foundation, sharpening your mental acumen as you navigate the labyrinth of corporate America. Just as a skyscraper's structure needs pillars to hold it tall, your mind requires stimulation and novelty to thrive. Reading serves as the ultimate brain workout, pushing your mental boundaries, and enhancing your cognitive faculties. With each page turned, you flex your intellectual muscles, forging new neural pathways and fostering an unyielding capacity for strategic thinking and innovation.

Now, let's dive into how this reading technique seamlessly complements the *skyscraper method*. You see, networking in the high-stakes realm of corporate America is akin to building connections between skyscraper floors. The more robust your connections, the more resilient your career tower becomes. Reading, my friend, propels your networking endeavors to a whole new dimension. As you consume books, your communication skills naturally evolve. You become adept at articulating complex ideas with clarity and elegance, a skill that's the hallmark of a master builder in the *skyscraper method*.

Picture yourself at a networking event where you effortlessly engage in an invigorating dialogue with a high-ranking executive. The words flow like a well-designed blueprint, revealing your deep-seated knowledge and confidence. Your well-versed arguments spark a lively debate, leading to a genuine exchange

of ideas. The outcome? A connection forged through intellectual camaraderie, a bond that extends far beyond mere business interactions.

But the true magic lies in your ability to apply these newfound
ideas and perspectives from your reading escapades to your
networking pursuits. Imagine discussing the nuances of real
estate investments, drawing insights from the pages of a book
like "Rich Dad Poor Dad: Rich Dad's Guide to Investing." As
you engage in a stimulating discourse, you build a genuine
connection with your executive counterpart, transcending the
conventional small talk. This connection doesn't fade away; it
thrives, fostering future collaborations and shared endeavors.

To succeed in this reading journey, it's crucial to select the right
books that align with your short-term goals and ambitions. Just
as a skyscraper's design must be meticulously chosen to fulfill
its purpose, your reading choices should resonate with your
career aspirations. Research, explore snippets, delve into rat-
ings, and peruse comments to ensure the books you choose are
a true match for your knowledge quest.

In the grand narrative of success, reading is your secret
weapon, wielded by some of the greatest minds of our time.
Icons like Elon Musk and Bill Gates, who devour a library's
worth of books annually, attest to the transformative power of
this habit. They sift through the sea of literature, selectively
seeking the wisdom that fuels their professional endeavors. It's
no coincidence that the likes of Gates read around 50 books a
year, viewing this practice as a constant source of inspiration
and growth.

So, my fellow aspiring skyscraper builders, seize the opportunity to enrich your mind and revolutionize your career. Embrace the challenge of reading at least one book per month, a goal well within reach with the right strategy. And remember, just as Bruce Lee embodied the adaptability of water, find your unique cadence for consuming knowledge, whether it's through traditional reading or embracing audiobooks during daily routines.

In the realm of networking and corporate triumphs, reading isn't a luxury – it's an investment, a potent force that enhances your intellectual arsenal. Every book you consume is another floor in your skyscraper of expertise, bolstering your ability to communicate, connect, and conquer in the vibrant landscape of corporate America. So, my ambitious friend, pick up that book, and open your mind!

Career in Action Activity: Elevate your Mind in 3 days

If you find yourself having read fewer than three non-fiction books over the past year (excluding fiction and academic reads), then this challenge is tailor-made for you.

Step 1: **Build Your Book Wish List**

Head over to the Appendix and explore my personal book list. Allow your curiosity to roam freely and compile your very own book wish list. Think about those intriguing subjects that you've always wanted to know more about.

Career in Action Activity: Elevate your Mind in 3 days *(cont)*

Step 2: **Select one book from the list**

Zero in on the topics that hold the key to your growth. The realm of possibilities is boundless – from negotiation tactics that could reshape your career trajectory, to mastering the art of public speaking, or even penning your own literary masterpiece. As you read, channel the Bruce Lee Mentality, extracting wisdom and techniques that resonate with your aspirations.

Step 3: **Three Chapters, Three Days**

Now, here's where the challenge kicks in. I dare you to pick a single book from your newly minted wish list. Over the course of three days, immerse yourself in this literary adventure by conquering three chapters. It might sound like a small commitment, but the impact is bound to be monumental. Track your thoughts, insights, and mental shifts as you absorb the wisdom on those pages.

These three chapters will serve as the cornerstone for your intellectual ascent.

Extra Credit: Embark on a Reading Journey
But why stop at just three chapters? For those who truly seek mastery, here's your chance for extra credit. Pace yourself, committing to complete one book each month. Set a short-term goal, dedicating the next 30 days to devouring the selected book. Once you've conquered this milestone, elevate your ambition to the next level – challenge yourself to conquer 12 books in 12 months.

> **Career in Action Activity: Elevate your Mind in 3 days *(cont)***
>
> Stay on track by joining forces with a book club or enlisting the support of an accountability partner. Remember, your reading journey will lay the foundation for a sharper, more agile mind that's primed to ascend the corporate landscape.

The act of reading isn't just an isolated exercise; it's an integral part of the process – a technique that breathes life into your tower of professional aspirations.

In the upcoming chapter, prepare to uncover three distinctive pathways to give back: through your time, your resources, and your knowledge. Each avenue is a mirror to the *skyscraper method's* phases, and just like a skyscraper's foundation and finishing touches, giving back reinforces the entirety of your career-building journey.

Chapter 15:
Give Back

"Gratitude is a currency for success"- Shaka Smart- American men's college basketball coach

Every step you've taken in your career, every milestone reached, every opportunity seized – they're all based on generosity. Each achievement, whether it was a door opened, a mentor's guidance, or a helping hand extended, has its roots in the powerful act of giving. It's a universal truth – anything earned, received, or achieved has been shaped by someone's willingness to bestow a gift upon you.

Reflect on your journey; you'll find moments where someone's choice to support you, to believe in you, changed your trajectory. Those instances of kindness, the moments where you were chosen, should resonate as beacons of gratitude, urging you to reciprocate the gift to another.

For me, it all started with Isabella Issac, a towering figure in the world of marketing. She held the title of Director of Marketing for a Lower Manhattan firm. And then there was me – a contractor on her event marketing team, just embarking on my post-graduation adventure. That 10-week contract was a pivotal juncture in my life, and little did I know the seeds of giving back were being sown.

Ms. Issac and I shared a rapport, a camaraderie built on shared laughs and musings about the impact of our team's efforts on the firm's success. But as my contract's final week loomed, I was facing an abyss – a potential stint of joblessness. The desperation weighed heavy, and I knew I had to summon every ounce of courage. So, I invited her to lunch, my heart pounding in my chest, and launched a Hail Mary – a plea for a permanent job on her team. Her gracious response caught me off guard; she extended a temporary position, month-to-month. Ecstasy washed over me – my back was off that jobless wall, at least temporarily. Eight months later, I had carved a name as a diligent worker and landed a permanent role on a different team.

Today, years have flown by like chapters in a book, and I stand at the threshold of wisdom. Isabella's kindness, her act of giving, echoes through my life as a guiding principle. I find myself paying it forward, imparting the wisdom of gratitude to another young, ambitious soul seeking a better life. You see, I've absorbed a profound truth – gratitude isn't just an emotion; it's the very currency of success. I repeat, gratitude is the currency for success. It's what propelled me forward, and now, it surges through me, propelling me to reach greater heights.

In this chapter, let's unveil the profound significance of giving back. Prepare to enhance your networking prowess and amplify the efficacy of the *skyscraper method* by embracing this practice. When you learn to give back, you're not just building connections; you're constructing bridges of purpose and impact.

As you channel your time, resources, and knowledge into causes beyond your immediate circle, you're forging links with kindred spirits who resonate with your values and aspirations. This isn't just about transactional exchanges; it's about co-creating a narrative of shared purpose, a story where your act of giving becomes an integral chapter in your career's saga.

We'll cover three dynamic ways of generosity – giving your time, leveraging your resources, and sharing your knowledge. Each avenue aligns harmoniously with the *skyscraper method*, bolstering your journey through assessment, planning, building, servicing, and now, giving back.

Give Your Time

Time – it's the currency of existence, the one resource we all share, and how we invest it is a testament to our priorities. Every tick of the clock shapes our lives, and in the realm of career development, how we choose to allocate our time can make all the difference. Now, imagine if I told you that by giving your time, you're not just investing in others; you're laying a cornerstone for your skyscraper of success.

Volunteering is more than a selfless act; it's a gateway to personal growth and meaningful connection. As you dedicate your time to a cause that resonates with your values, you're sowing the seeds of gratitude and forging bonds that reach far beyond the task at hand. This reciprocity is the hidden gem of giving – as you enrich the lives of others, you find fulfillment echoing back to you.

Consider that volunteering isn't a one-way street. It's a nexus where the giver and the recipient meet, and the reverberations extend beyond that moment. The community benefits, you benefit, and your career benefits. Yes, you read that right – dedicating your time can actually propel your professional trajectory.

Let's break it down further, shall we? By stepping into the role of a volunteer, you're not just offering a helping hand; you're also opening doors to new connections. Whether it's rubbing elbows with fellow volunteers or mingling with community members during a project, you're expanding your network in a profound way. And here's the kicker – this isn't your typical networking event. It's genuine, it's authentic, and it's bound by the shared purpose of making a difference.

And if you're a newcomer to a city, volunteering becomes your ultimate ally. My own experience stands testament to this truth. The time spent at a local soup kitchen not only warmed hearts through acts of service but also introduced my wife and me to a tribe of like-minded professionals. In the space of just three months, we'd broadened our professional network.

But it gets better – volunteering serves as a playground for personal and professional growth. Those skills you wield in the workplace – teamwork, leadership, problem-solving – find fertile ground in the realm of giving back. It's like an incubator for development, a space where you can test the waters, hone your skills, and build a reservoir of confidence.

Picture this scenario: you volunteer with an employee resource group (ERG) dedicated to advocacy. In this unique setting, you find yourself leading a team, navigating challenges, and crafting impactful solutions. This trial by fire isn't just about giving; it's about evolving. As you refine your leadership style, the rewards are twofold – you're contributing to a noble cause while also nurturing skills that you can carry into your career.

And let's not forget the undeniable therapeutic benefits. Volunteering, like a soothing balm, shifts your perspective from self to others. It's a reminder of the basic needs we share and a realization that, in service, we find solace. The act of giving doesn't drain; it rejuvenates, reducing stress and illuminating the path to a more balanced, purposeful life.

So, giving back time is more than just a gesture; it's an investment in yourself. As you enrich lives and build connections, you're fortifying the very core of your career journey. The *skyscraper method's* foundation widens, the walls strengthen, and the pinnacle of your success gleams brighter, all because of the time you choose to give.

Leveraging Your Resources

If you're pressed for time and volunteering seems like a distant dream, fear not. There's another route to making a meaningful impact: donating resources. Consider contributing canned goods to homeless shelters, passing on gently used clothes to local nonprofits, equipping schools in need with supplies, or even directing funds back into your alma mater.

But here's the kicker: it's not a one-way street. Donating resources isn't just about the charity; it's about you too. It's about that warm feeling that spreads through you, knowing you've played a part in a cause that matters.

Now, think of it like this – remember when we talked about the essence of fulfillment during the Digging phase of the *Skyscraper method*? Well, donating resources is like another layer to that cake of fulfillment. It's about finding a cause that resonates with your core and backing it with your resources.

For instance, let me share a personal story. Back in the day, I benefited from resources donors gave to the local gym and churches. Which gave me access to sports and games – my life's classroom, teaching me skills I still use today – teamwork, determination, and goal-setting. Fast forward, and now I'm paying it forward. I'm providing resources like sports equipment, toys, and finances to local community organizations. It's a way of revisiting my youth and empowering kids who share my passion.

But it's not just about nostalgia; it's about purpose. I've set my sights on being a servant leader and supporting young black men. And guess what? Donating clothes to local nonprofits that align with this mission is my way of putting words into action.

So, consider donating resources. Your contributions, whether big or small, resonate beyond the surface, creating ripples of change that touch lives – including yours.

Sharing Your Knowledge

Another route to giving back is by sharing your hard-earned knowledge. No matter who you are, there's someone out there who could greatly benefit from what you've learned along your journey. Your wisdom might stem from career choices, school experiences, or honed skills that you've perfected through years of practice. All of it holds immense value, and it can be a beacon of guidance for those striving to reach where you stand today. So, why not extend a helping hand to someone in need? The beauty lies in the fact that you never truly know how your act of sharing could significantly impact someone's life. It has the power to reshape perspectives and potentially change the course of another's destiny. And let me tell you, one of the most impactful ways I've discovered to share knowledge is through the art of mentorship.

Throughout the years, I've taken on the role of mentor, guiding high school students through college choices, helping college students map their career paths, assisting early-career professionals in finding their true callings, aiding mid-level professionals in network building, and supporting senior executives in transitioning careers. You see, sharing knowledge isn't just an act of altruism; it's a conduit to profound personal fulfillment. This form of servant leadership circles back to my core mission, aligning seamlessly with the essence of who I am.

Now, let's delve into a real-world mentoring scenario. Picture a mentee wrestling with a challenge, using a strategy that, from your seasoned perspective, you know won't cut it. Perhaps they're stumbling through unsuccessful job interviews. In such instances, you take them through the steps of the Framing Phase. By unveiling their C.L.E.A.R. career goals, you pave the way for a solid action plan. Together, you navigate towards roles that not only spark their passion but also involve strategic networking within the industry. The result? Your mentee gains the inside track before even applying, leading to a remarkable uptick in their interview success rate. It's a classic win-win.

Mentorship isn't just about what you bestow; it's about what you receive in return. When you lend an attentive ear to your mentees, you open the door to fresh perspectives and innovative approaches. It's like being handed a key to a treasure trove of new insights. From innovative software to unconventional strategies, my interactions with mentees have enriched me personally and professionally.

Lastly, there's the pure joy of witnessing growth. Seeing a mentee flourish due to your guidance, observing them triumph in their career pursuits – that's a reward like no other. Plus, when faced with a mentee's challenges, you have the chance to brainstorm alternative solutions and fine-tune processes, often resulting in remarkable turnarounds.

Here's a prime example. I once mentored an individual grappling with the departure of senior teammates. Without them there was a lack of leadership, leaving her overwhelmed and underappreciated. She was considering a career change. I prompted her to envision herself as the leader, the expert. This seemingly small shift sparked a major transformation. She not only reclaimed her role but also secured a substantial salary boost and the ability to lead her own team. Perspective, my friends, has the power to reshape destinies.

Another conduit for sharing knowledge is through content distribution. Think articles shared online or impactful books passed along. Imagine gifting a copy of this transformative book to a student, young professional, or colleague. It's not just about suggesting they get it; it's about taking that extra step purchasing *Skyscraper: A Proven Method To Build A Dream Career* to invest in their growth.

So, here's my rallying call to you: open your heart to extending a hand to others. The act of giving back is an elixir for personal fulfillment, igniting passion and fueling your journey through *the Skyscraper Method*. I can attest to the unparalleled rush of gratitude that accompanies volunteering, donating, and mentoring. And I sincerely hope that you, too, will join me on this fulfilling journey. Your contributions have the potential to shape destinies and spark transformations. Together, we'll create a ripple effect of positive change, leaving an indelible mark on the lives we touch.

Career in Action Activity: Give Back and Make a Difference

Now that we've journeyed through the realms of giving back, it's time to put these principles into action. Cast your gaze upon the non-profit organizations that thread through your community's fabric or have a direct impact on your loved ones. Create a concise list and delve into some research about the tangible influence each organization wields. Then, take the plunge and lend your support to at least one of these non-profits. Whether it's offering your time, resources, or knowledge, you're embarking on a path that leads to an immeasurable wellspring of fulfillment.

Feeling a bit uncertain about where to begin? No worries. Here are a few suggestions to follow as you embark on this impactful journey:

- **Soup Kitchens:** These hubs of nourishment not only feed the body but also the soul of the community. Volunteering here can offer a heartwarming experience.
- **Employee Resource Groups:** Often overlooked, these groups can be an unexpected source of connection and support, both for you and those you aim to assist.
- **Libraries or Senior Centers:** These cultural hubs offer a treasure trove of opportunities to engage and uplift the community, especially its elder members.

Career in Action Activity: Give Back and Make a Difference *(cont)*

- **Youth Organizations and After-School Programs:** Channel your passion for growth and development by getting involved in programs that shape the next generation.
- **Homeless Shelters and Rescue Organizations:** Extend your hand to those in need by contributing to shelters or organizations that work tirelessly to provide shelter and care.
- **Local Animal Shelters:** For the animal lovers among us, these shelters are a haven for furry friends awaiting a loving home.
- **Places of Worship:** Churches, synagogues, and similar places of worship often spearhead initiatives that benefit the community. Your involvement can be a source of solace and support.

Remember, this is just the tip of the iceberg. The journey of giving back is as diverse as the communities we serve. So, step forward, dive in, and watch as your act of kindness sets off ripples of positive change, not only in the lives you touch but also within your own heart and soul.

As you stand on the edge of the final chapter – the Grand Opening – the culmination of your efforts comes into focus. Just as a skyscraper's grand opening marks the culmination of meticulous planning and relentless execution, your journey through this book mirrors the stages of construction. You've excavated the foundation of self-awareness, laid the bricks of networking, and adorned it with the elegance of giving back.

Now, as you turn the page to the Grand Opening, prepare to step into the spotlight. This is the moment where you'll unveil your career's grand vision, shining a light on the monumental achievement you've been crafting. With the curtain about to rise on this closing act.

▶ Phase 8: The Grand Opening!

Skyscraper Method

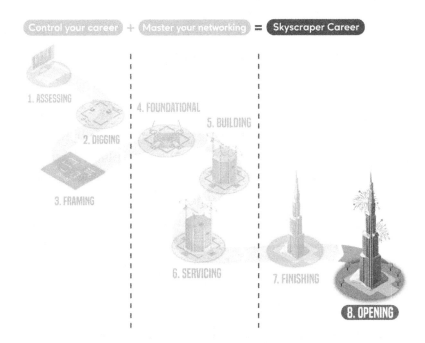

Control your career + Master your networking = Skyscraper Career

1. ASSESSING
2. DIGGING
3. FRAMING
4. FOUNDATIONAL
5. BUILDING
6. SERVICING
7. FINISHING
8. OPENING

Today's marks the unveiling of a new city landmark- a soaring skyscraper that stands as a testament to resilience, designed with personal touch that adds character to the skyline. The lavish grand opening ceremony is about to begin, starting with the fireworks, followed by the cutting of the red ribbon- your very own skyscraper is complete. Congratulations! With this accomplishment, you now wield the power to shape your career based on passion and master the art of professional networking. This journey has been a profound one, marked by transformations you've embraced for the sake of your career. Applause is in order! As we close this book, we return to its inception- the seed that sprouted the *skyscraper method*. The story serves to inspire you with its simplicity, remind you of the influential connections within your reach, and prove that your dream career is attainable. If I can achieve it, so can you.

How did I land five job offers in just five days?

I navigated a path built on Visibility - Credibility- Trust. I mastered the art of cultivation, focusing on relationship-building. By nurturing these connections, I planted seeds of trust among key influencers, reaping the rewards of quick career opportunities precisely when I needed them most. The outcome? A remarkable five verbal job offers presented to me in the span of just one week. But, let's rewind a bit – the journey's origins were anything but extraordinary.

And so, here's how it all unfolded:

The most groundbreaking episode of my career transpired at a juncture when everything seemed at its lowest point. It was during one of those routine weekly sit-downs with my manager, where the air held an unusual tension. I occupied my usual spot in his office, ready to provide my updates. But before I could even begin, he interjected abruptly: "Timothy, I've got some unsettling news. Brace yourself. The project you've been pouring your energy into? It's been axed." The weight of it hit me like a freight train – months of toil and sweat down the drain. And to compound the blow, he dropped another bombshell: "Leadership's made the call – all resources for the project, gone." I was shocked; I had just completed a significant overhaul and was in the groove as a process designer.

With a calculated silence, he slid an ominous "white folder" across the desk. Its glossy surface glinted under the office lights, a stark contrast to the impending revelation. Trembling hands reached out, and as I flipped it open, the contents revealed themselves. My eyes scanned over my work history, and the cold, form letters of "parting ways" hammered home the reality. Wait a second – "parting ways"? It hit me like a ton of bricks – I was staring at my severance package.

Amidst a maelstrom of emotions, I summoned a poker face, determined to keep my composure. But beneath that veneer, a storm brewed. Anger simmered, fueled by the injustice of being laid off. A barrage of questions stormed my mind, relentless and unyielding. *Why me? How could I continue providing for my family? What led me down this path in the first place? What was my next move?* A whirlwind of confusion and betrayal engulfed me, yet I managed a smile, extending gratitude for the opportunity, and with my head held high, I exited his office, the weight of the world lingering.

Once out of his sight, I hurried to my cubicle, desperation gripping me. A quick call to my wife was the next step, my voice conveying the magnitude of the situation. With urgency, I detailed the turn of events, sketching out my blueprint to secure an equivalent position. My wife, a product of Chicago's formidable South Side, a place that hardens those who call it home, offered unwavering assurance: "I believe in you, baby. Trust that we're covered. Do whatever it takes."

The "Bat Phone Plan"

At that moment, I realized it was time to activate what I affectionately called the "Bat Phone Plan."

It's a concept drawn from those iconic scenes in '80s Batman episodes – the Gotham commissioner reaching for the red phone, summoning Batman in times of dire need. Welp, I was in dire need, so I embarked on a humbling journey. I tapped into my professional network, reaching out to those I'd cultivated relationships with. It was a lifeline I cast, a signal for aid in times of uncertainty. While success was never guaranteed, I held faith that these connections would respond promptly, opening doors to potential opportunities and recommending me for roles within the company. I was ready to rely on my severance package if push came to shove, but before that, my metaphorical "bat phone" lit up.

In essence, I became the commissioner of my own professional Gotham, forging connections with precision, each interaction serving as a resonant note in a symphony of strategic networking.

Stay tuned as I unveil the cast of characters who heeded my call, leaping into action to salvage my professional trajectory from the abyss.

1. The Previous Manager

You know the adage – never burn bridges? Well, that principle held true in my past experience. In a previous role, my manager bore witness to my success executing deliverables and recognized my raw talent. Our connection grew over time, cultivated through mutual respect. Eventually, after a productive two years, I ventured onward, seeking a more promising position. While our direct collaboration ceased, I remained steadfast in maintaining the bridge we had built. Like clockwork, every quarter, I rekindled that connection. Our conversations bridged personal and professional realms, weaving a strong bond. Fate would have it that our paths would cross again – the very day after my encounter with the dreaded "white folder."

It was during this pivotal touchpoint that I unveiled my predicament, recounting the emergency that had befallen me. The response was nothing short of extraordinary. My former manager revealed an open role within his team – a role that would soon become one of the five verbal offers that graced my inbox. His words, etched in clarity, resonated: "If you're open to the idea of returning, we can absolutely make it a reality."

And there you have it – one offer secured, with four more poised on the horizon. The journey was just beginning.

2. The Current Manager

In an unforeseen twist, the manager who laid me off earlier that morning, called me back into his office that same day. I was confused. *What does he want now?* I reluctantly walked back to his office, but I walked in with a smile on my face. You might be thinking, why did I have a positive attitude while being laid off? It was all because of Mark Cuban.

In the early 2000s, the owner of the Dallas Mavericks, Mark Cuban, had a reality TV show called *The Benefactor*. I'm an NBA fanatic, so the show gave me a behind the scene look at how an NBA owner operated. Think Donald Trump's, *The Apprentice*, but the contestants competed for a C-suite job in Cuban's empire. Among the final two contenders, a pivotal challenge emerged – How would they react upon learning of their rival's victory.

In this high-stakes showdown they gave both contestants bad news, then judged their reaction from losing to the other contestant. The first losing contestant used a lot of colorful expletives behind closed doors, berating Cuban and the show. Whereas, the other losing contestant reacted was humble and thankful for the experience behind closed doors. Pretty obvious, who one that last challenge, and thereby the competition–the humble contestant.

Now, as I sat in that office, the memory of that humble contestant reverberated in my mind. It struck me – I should leave a mark of gratitude and thankfulness. So despite the bad news I kept a positive attitude. My former manager took note and mentioned my reaction. Amidst the sea of colleagues released that day, I stood out – a memorable response. As a result, he extended me an unexpected olive branch, offering a junior role on another team. He recognized it was below my experience level, yet he presented it as a gesture of goodwill, a temporary role until I could find a better opportunity. The weight of the burden of joblessness began lifting off of my shoulders. *My career isn't over.*

At that moment, I offered a genuine smile, thanked him for the connection, indicated I'd contemplate the offer, sealed our interaction with a firm handshake, and walked out of his office with newfound optimism.

That's two verbal offers, let's continue!

3. The Interviewer

Several influencers in my networking life cycle come from cultivating relationships with former interviewers. Have you ever realized mid-interview that the role you're up for is *not* for you? Maybe the role is seeking a more experienced candidate or the technology that this team uses is unfamiliar and you're not interested in learning a new tool, but the bottom line is you discover that you're not interested anymore. In these situations, I don't get discouraged or think of the interview as a waste of time. I try to turn the set back into an opportunity to build a rapport with the interviewer. Especially when it's a job I'm interested in. And if I get a sense that this person could be a great mentor, I ask for a follow-up conversation and then convert that interview into a recurring touch point.

One such instance, I sustained a relationship with an interviewer from a consulting firm. In the interview we got off topic and got in an engaging discussion around the polarizing perspectives of consultant agencies. We both shared stories and had a good laugh. Even though I didn't have the experience to secure the job, I leveraged our interview into a lasting business relationship. We started meeting quarterly and built a strong professional relationship. Adding this interviewer into my networking life cycle. And It paid off! After receiving the dreaded "white envelope" I reached out to this manager seeking opportunities in his division, he had two open roles that I could start immediately.

Three relationships, four job offers!

4. The Former Colleague

I had a great working relationship with a more senior colleague. We had collaborated on a few projects and she had always given me great advice. Over two years, our bond transformed into a peer-mentor relationship, and we talked regularly about personal and professional topics. My objective in these interactions was to showcase not just my hard work ethic but also my collaborative spirit.

After the layoff, I reached out to her, leaving a voicemail with my concerns. She responded that evening. We talked about the situation, and in an instant, she recommended a role she had insight into, facilitating an email introduction with the hiring manager. Endorsing my work ethic and ambitions, she gave me a glowing recommendation. Merely two days later, I found myself face-to-face with the hiring manager. The open position mirrored my current one, offering me a platform to dazzle the hiring manager with my project management skills. By the end of our chat he said "I can see why you got such a stellar recommendation. If you'd like the role, it's yours!"

And there it was- Breakthrough! I secured five verbal job offers in five days, for positions that I didn't even apply to and after the most challenging day of my career. The speed of this second chance took me by surprise, and the swift response of those I reached out to left me amazed. The bat phone plan worked! My professional path was reset for a fresh trajectory. The spectrum of the five opportunities spanned across various business domains – Risk, Finance, Technology, and Product. The next step was a weighty decision. *Which job should I choose?*

Before the layoff, I had crafted a personal mission statement that encapsulated my passions, though I kept it guarded, even placing a printed copy on my desk without sharing it. Simultaneously, I fostered relationships with influential figures I admired, nurturing these connections through candid discussions encompassing both work and life. Unbeknownst to me, I had already laid the groundwork for the *skyscraper method*. The layoff served as a catalyst, prompting a fresh perspective on career hunting, and I posed a series of questions to myself: *Do I truly comprehend my passions? Haven't I cultivated strong relationships with executives? Why not merge these connections with roles that align with my passions?* It was at that moment that the seed of the *skyscraper method* took root.

At this juncture, my pre-layoff personal mission statement played its role. I listed the roles, pitted them against my mission statement, and cut the unsuitable ones. After my analysis, there was only one job that allowed me to do what I love: solve problems. This led me to the risk management role, the one referred to me by my former colleague.

Success! In just five business days following my receipt of a pink slip – or in my case, a glossy white folder – as I seamlessly transitioned into a new position with comparable compensation. My career trajectory remained unhindered, propelling me closer to my purpose and ensuring the well-being of my family. This realization fostered a deep sense of gratitude for my connections and fortified my confidence in my career journey.

Within the risk role, I embarked on a journey of learning and growth, absorbing insights into investment products and connecting with new leaders to add to my networking lifecycle. In retrospect, the layoff wasn't just a setback; it was an opportunity to recalibrate, to leverage my connections for meaningful job pursuits, and to base my career choices on genuine passion rather than vague job descriptions. A path that eliminated the uncertainties of the interview process, replacing them with insights from within. Ever since, this vetting approach has guided my career course, fostering a deeper love for what I do today.

Receiving all those offers in such a short span was surreal and effortless. I hadn't anticipated the extent to which my professional network would rally to support my job search. I had, in essence, underestimated the potency of the relationships I had nurtured. Effortlessly, my severance package acted as a catalyst, prompting them into action and bestowing upon me fresh opportunities.

Receiving those five offers wasn't just a random sequence of events – it symbolized the *skyscraper method* in action. I took control to steer my career path into Risk, entwining it with superior networking, these five offers marked the beginning of my grand opening.

Sky's the Limit

Today, as I pen down these words, many years have passed since my layoff, yet the lessons I learned remain etched in my mind. My hope is that my story ignites a fire within you, propelling you toward your dream career with an unwavering determination.

From that grand opening moment, I've honed my networking skills, fine-tuning my approach to engage with influencers who align with my "C.L.E.A.R." goals. My professional network has since surged, comprising numerous executives I know personally and professionally. What's even more gratifying is that I've empowered countless mentees and clients with the method, witnessing their careers skyrocket. Transitioning from innovation to career development, I've found my niche as a part-time career coach, sharing the *skyscraper method* and offering unwavering accountability. Remarkable results have fueled my desire to one day do this full time, as I've witnessed professionals discover their passion and pivot into careers they adore. I hope the same for you.

Perhaps you picked up this book because your career path feels elusive, or you're keen to master the art of networking. Questions about your career's direction might be gnawing at you: *"Why did I choose this path? Where do I see myself? Who supports my journey?"* Trust me, I get it – the struggle was all too real when I first stepped into the corporate world.

It's time to rewrite your narrative. The beauty of the *Skyscraper method* lies in its simplicity, offering exercises that yield tangible results. My wish is that you reflect on your career's trajectory. You shouldn't need a layoff, like I did, to inaugurate the grand opening of your skyscraper. Avoid being pushed into that corner; seize control by pursuing your passions and networking fervently now. The tips I've shared are your playbook for career triumph. Take action, uncover roles that resonate with your heart, and construct a network that secures those positions. Once accomplished, revisit the career health check in Phase 1 – the answer should be a resounding "Yes" to every question. I want you to work with unparalleled passion, steering your career's trajectory at will. Forge abundant connections, both personal and professional. Consequently, like my clients, be privy to job opportunities that align with your passions ahead of the curve, capitalizing on chances to boost your income.

The time has come to relish your livelihood and be generously compensated for it. You might wonder, "What's my next move?" It's simple: First, immerse yourself in the Career in Action activities outlined in this book. This primes you to make the optimal corporate move. Second, reach out to me – yes, you heard me right – reach out to me, at my company Careers in Action LLC. I yearn to grasp the true impact of this book on you and your career journey. You'll find my contact information in the appendix. Don't hesitate; drop me a message and share your story. I'm eager to witness how my *skyscraper method* fuels your corporate success.

If you're interested in working together, I offer an array of career development workshops, one-on-one coaching sessions, interview preparation, resume reviews, career planning, negotiations, and more. I'm here to challenge your perspective on your career's past and future. Together, we'll delve into your passions, validate your C.L.E.A.R. goals; furnish you with networking tools, and ensure your accountability. My ultimate desire is for you to thrive in a career that resonates deeply and pays handsomely.

I'm just a kid from Brownsville, Brooklyn, who stumbled upon a method to relish the fruits of corporate America. I find joy in my job, boasting a network of leaders who propel my growth, earning enough to support my family, and savoring life's everyday wonders. I wish the same for you and those you hold dear. This book's essence is encapsulated in the words of my hometown's legendary lyricist, Notorious B.I.G.: "Stay far from timid, only make moves when your heart is in it. Live one phrase, Sky's the limit." To me, this statement signifies that action within the realms of our passions holds no bounds for our careers. See you at the top!

Epilogue:
A Journey Through the
Skyscraper Method

My journey recounted here predates the creation of the *Skyscraper methodology*. Looking back, I now realize that I inadvertently followed each of the phases outlined in this book, which paved the path to my desired career. Allow me to share, highlighting each phase as I progress through the story:

My entry into the corporate world was through a rotational program shortly after completing Business school (B-School). For those unfamiliar, a rotational program is an initiative that many companies employ to provide fresh talent with diverse work experiences over a defined time span. Typically spanning two years, these programs expose recent graduates to various roles before they settle into a specific position within the organization. My participation focused on a variation where recent graduates rotated through different roles without a long-term commitment, aiming for both personal growth and a mutually beneficial company-employee match.

This may sound idyllic, but my reality was far from joyful.

From the outset, my experience sucked! After seven months in my initial rotation, the disparity between my career aspirations and actual experience was glaring (Phase #1). To complicate matters, the program's location requirements necessitated a move from D.C. to Charlotte, North Carolina. This geographical shift compounded the challenges of adjusting to a new city and restarting in a different job.

My daily tasks felt mundane, uninspiring, and stressful, creating a toxic blend of boredom and career uncertainty. The workplace boredom coupled with anxiety over my professional future was a recipe for unhappiness. I dreaded every day at the office. The team I was a part of felt disjointed, leaving me doubting not only my choice of company but also my decision to pursue a graduate degree and relocate. It was an all-around miserable situation, prompting thoughts of quitting and returning to my hometown of Brooklyn. At that time, had I assessed my career using a "career health check" (Phase #1), I would have likened myself to a tent – a fragile career built on lack of control and mere tolerance for the job's financial rewards. My networking endeavors were feeble, as I lacked the confidence to engage with others.

However, a single day changed everything. During an extended workshop, as executives introduced their teams to newly minted MBA graduates, one speaker stood out. In a strong New York City accent, a charismatic voice boomed, "My name is TJ. I'm from Queens, NY, where we say, 'Fugetaboutit!'" Instantly captivated, I sat up straight. TJ exuded an aura that was hard to ignore. His presentation was engaging, clear, and direct. His transformation team tackled innovative consumer products, answering the question, "What's next?" – a concept I resonated with due to my interest in simplifying new technologies for widespread use. It was as if the clouds obscuring my career path had suddenly cleared, revealing a job that I could genuinely enjoy. Subconsciously, I linked TJ's mission with my own (Phase #2). Although I hadn't formalized a "personal mission statement" back then, I recognized the alignment between his team's work and my own aspirations. During my time in graduate school, I had developed a passion for creating business cases and had even volunteered to teach undergraduates how to create them. TJ's presentation invigorated me, breathing life into my work after months of stagnation. I knew I had to be part of his team (Phase #3).

As the workshop concluded, a new fire burned within me. Meeting TJ became my priority, making him my number one target for mentorship (Phase #4). Approaching him nervously after the conference, I initiated a memorable introduction: "Hello TJ! I'm Timothy Nurse, hailing from the finest borough, Brooklyn! Despite your allegiance to the Yankees via Queens and my devotion to the Mets, I'd love to connect and learn about your work." He responded with a warm smile and a hearty affirmation. Suppressing my inner excitement, I maintained composure, shook his hand, and obtained his email address.

After connecting with his assistant, we eventually met for lunch a few months later (Phase #5). Over the course of our conversation, I introduced a beta version of my "Hello Slide" (Phase #4) and shared my aspiration to extract greater value from the rotational program. During our discussion, I mentioned my experience playing college basketball, leading to a serendipitous connection: TJ's 11-year-old son needed a basketball skills coach. I eagerly volunteered (Phase #7) and spent the following months coaching his son's team on fundamental basketball techniques. Through these interactions, TJ and I delved deeper into our shared passions (Phase #2) and my career expectations (Phase #3). Our out-of-office conversations surpassed the impact of standard in-office networking meetings, fostering a stronger and more accelerated connection.

This ongoing rapport resulted in TJ selecting me for his transformation team during my final rotation in the program. Finally, I was engaged in work that resonated with my interests. Over the course of an eight-month period, I attended a golf fundraiser hosted by TJ, where I had a fateful encounter with Nelson – the affable Midwesterner with a penchant for cigars, whom you might recall from Chapter 12: Networking Life Cycle. This meeting completed a satisfying circle of connections.

My narrative could have ended with my newfound happiness, but several years later, after leaving the rotational program, I found myself in an uninspiring project management role. During this period, I immersed myself in Stephen Covey's "7 Habits of Highly Effective People" (Phase #7), developed a refined "personal mission statement" (Phase #2), and identified my true career passion – innovation (Phase #3). It was during a bi-annual meeting with Nelson (Phase #5) that fate intervened. As I presented my "snapshot slide" (Phase #4), I voiced my desire to transition into a role focused on innovative business cases. To my delight, Nelson offered his assistance, providing the contact information of a colleague seeking talent for a new innovations team. With that name in hand, I took the initiative to send a cold email, referencing Nelson's endorsement.

The leader of this new innovation team replied promptly. A subsequent conversation led to a presentation of my perfected "Hello Slide" (Phase #4), and we discovered numerous personal and professional commonalities – shared interests in the New York Jets, extensive project management experience, and a passion for innovation.

Within a week, my updated resume was requested (Phase #1), and a new role tailored to my skills was created on his team – a role I embraced with eagerness. I transitioned seamlessly, thriving in the innovation space thanks to my well-cultivated network. This is the embodiment of the *Skyscraper method* at work. Networking with TJ initiated a rotational role, which led to my introduction to Nelson. By consistently nurturing my relationship with Nelson, I felt comfortable expressing my career aspirations, culminating in an ideal job offer. Within a month, I transitioned from a dissatisfying project management role to a fulfilling innovation career, which I've now embraced for five years.

The most satisfying part of this narrative is that my journey extended beyond me. Through the expression of my passions and consistent networking efforts, I began receiving exclusive insights into upcoming job openings. This "insider information" provided me with a safety net and the ability to help my peers by sharing potential job opportunities before they were made public. This added security was invaluable, assuring me that I wouldn't be without options, even in uncertain times.

Furthermore, I've extended my success to others by coaching them on the *Skyscraper method*, consistently witnessing transformative results. By following these phases, my clients have unlocked their potential, cultivated robust networks, and secured their dream careers. My ultimate aspiration is for you to embrace *the Skyscraper method* and embark on your journey towards building the career of your dreams.

Appendix

Chapter 4: Resume/LinkedIn Checklist

General Resume & LinkedIn Tips:

- Master the CCC Rule: When reviewing your resume, read it aloud without pausing. This ensures clarity and helps you catch any grammatical errors. Don't underestimate the power of spell check and autocorrect to keep your resume error-free. And remember, if you can express something in fewer words, do it! Conciseness is key.

- Harness the Power of Keywords: Recognize that employers often use scanning software to filter through job applications. Be strategic in describing your qualifications and skills, using relevant keywords that will maximize the impact of your resume.

- Flip the Chronology: Arrange your work history in reverse chronological order, starting with your most recent job at the top. This allows recruiters to see your most recent experiences and achievements first, giving them a clear picture of your career progression.

- Craft Descriptive Bullets: Collaborate with a trusted friend or mentor to fine-tune the bullets in your work history section. Each bullet should follow the formula of action, situation, and result. For example, start with an action verb like "Led," then describe the situation or project you worked on, and conclude by highlighting the positive outcome you achieved.

- Embrace the Power of Verbs: The first word after each bullet point should always be an action verb. Use past tense verbs for previous roles and present tense verbs for your current job. Remember, if you're struggling to find a verb to start your bullet point, don't shy away from using one! Verbs create a sense of action and grab recruiters' attention.

- Showcase Applicable Skills: If you have a dedicated skills section, focus on listing skills and technologies that align with your job achievements. Avoid the temptation to include an exhaustive list of every product in a software suite. Instead, mention overarching skills such as "Microsoft Office Suite" to demonstrate your proficiency.

Resume Checklist:

- Craft a Concise Summary: For those with a small paragraph at the beginning of their resume, describe yourself in one powerful sentence. Capture your essence and make a memorable impression from the start.

- Protect Your Privacy: Only include essential personal details like your name and email address. Adding a LinkedIn URL is acceptable, but home addresses and personal phone numbers are no longer necessary. Keep your focus on professional information.

- Prioritize Recent Experience: Ensure that your latest job receives the most attention and detail in your resume. Highlight your growth in responsibilities over the years. Remember, the last job should have fewer bullet points, allowing your most recent accomplishments to shine.

- Maintain Font Consistency: Choose a professional font such as Times New Roman, Arial, or Calibri and stick with it throughout your resume. Fancy fonts may be too distracting. Consistency in font choice reflects a polished and professional image.

- Embrace Aesthetic Appeal: Your resume should resemble a perfectly tailored suit. Print it out or save it as a PDF and view it on your phone to assess its alignment, including dates, titles, and bullets. Ensure everything looks visually appealing and well-organized.

- Opt for Simplicity: Stick with plain white paper when printing your resume. Some may attempt to stand out with colored paper, heavy textures, or unique choices, but it doesn't give you an advantage. Recruiters are more interested in the content of your resume than the paper type.

- Keep it to One Page: I strongly recommend limiting your resume to a single page. Recruiters become frustrated when they have to sift through multiple pages per candidate, especially in high-demand situations. Consider consolidating or removing work experience from over 10 years ago. Focus on optimizing your resume's content to fit within one page for maximum impact.

By implementing these resume strategies, you'll create a powerful and visually appealing document that captures recruiters' attention, effectively presents your qualifications, and enhances your chances of success in the competitive job market.

LinkedIn Checklist:

- Perfect Your Profile Picture: Choose a high-resolution professional headshot for your LinkedIn profile. A compelling photo adds credibility and brings your profile to life. You can also personalize your profile by adding a cover photo as a background to your headshot.

- Showcase Your Portfolio: If applicable, include snippets of externally permitted projects you've completed or articles you've published. Make sure they represent high-quality work that you can be proud of. Always confirm with the relevant companies or publications before sharing.
- Seek Recommendations: Reach out to former colleagues on LinkedIn who have worked with you on notable projects and request recommendations. These short notes of recognition from your connections add validity to your value as a professional. When recruiters and other members view your profile, they'll see the positive impact you've had on others.
- Highlight Your Professional Journey: Take advantage of LinkedIn's platform to include comprehensive information about your professional experiences. If you need to condense information from your three-page resume, feel free to expand on the details within your LinkedIn page

By implementing the LinkedIn strategies, you'll enhance your online presence, establish credibility, and make a lasting impression on potential employers, clients, and professional connections. Your LinkedIn profile will serve as a powerful tool to showcase your expertise, achievements, and the positive impact you've made throughout your career

Chapter 4: Willie Sample Resume

WILLIE B. SMYTH
Atlanta, Gorgia, 30303 • 404.000.0000 • will.smith321@gmail.com

Creative thinker with experience in managing brands, driving sales, and building relationships

EXPERIENCE

BEL AIR TECHNOLOGY, Atlanta, GA   2022-Present
Associate Brand Manager- Global Enterprise Platforms Marketing
- Analyzed international competitor research, product development, and packaging design to identify market opportunities for new $60MM platform sub-line
- Evaluate domestic and international markets to create brand architecture education and communications, and analyze customer marketing touch points
- Lead brand liaison in development and execution of strategic partnership with Minor League Baseball. This effort impacts ~1 million customers and $60MM annual transactions

JOHNSON & JOHNSON, Atlanta, GA   2018-2020
Junior Brand Manager- Consumer Health Division
- Created unique Consumer Health hospitality experience for 100+ business clients and activated an integrated marketing program to support Tylenol products. Achieved 5MM total media element impressions and delivered 30MM PR impressions
- Optimized core Band-Aid product portfolio through i) in-depth analysis to identify opportunities and ii) leadership of project teams responsible for the development and execution of product platforms designed to capitalize on those opportunities

OGILVY & MATHER, New York, NY   Summer 2017
Advertising Summer Internship-
- Collaborated with agency partners in leading communications strategy, creative development, and execution for Key Drive Times and Single Serve business segment
- Led cross-functional team to develop and implement advertising campaigns for Delta Airlines, Ben & Jerry's, Miller Brewing Co., Turner South, Allstate, and Nike, representing ~50% of firm revenue

RALPH LAUREN, New York, NY   Summer 2016
Designer Summer Internship- Business Strategy Department
- Developed cost forecasting, tracked customer behavior, defined proof of concept, obtained user experience resources, and completed required product approvals
- Collaborated with stakeholders across Growth Marketing, Analytics, and Data Engineering teams to conceive, develop, implement, and maintain a new BI solution for tracking CPA and LTV of consumers.

CARMAX, Los Angeles, CA   2014-2016
Sales Consultant- Luxury Department
- Managed 2.3 MM book of business and Implemented incentive programs for sales team promoting financial services products

EDUCATION

HOWARD UNIVERSITY, Washington, DC   Graduation Date: 2022
School of Business- Master of Business Administration
- Concentration: Marketing and Corporate Strategy
- Vice President, Marketing Club

BANKS COLLEGE, Los Angeles, CA   Graduation Date: 2017
School of Business-Bachelor of Science
- Major: Business Administration, Minor: Marketing
- Academic Scholar, Member of Men's Basketball Team

ADDITIONAL

- Skills: Advanced MS Office, Agile, Spotfire, and working knowledge of SQL Toad
- Interests: Philanthropy, Golfing, Social Networking, Fitness, Photography

Chapter 5: Sample Personal Mission Statement

Character:

I will be a person who: Brings together family and friends. A humble loving man that gives back. A loving husband and father

Passion:

- What do I really love to do at work? Solve Problems, innovate with others, help others reach their potential
- What do I really love to do in my personal life? Play with kids, Date wife, sweat, listen to gospel, rap, and reggae

Imagination:

If I had unlimited time and resources, and knew I could not fail, what would I choose to do? I would: Purchase rental properties, coach others, open an outdoor gym, travel frequently, relax on a beach, spend time with my family, and visit friends

Vision:

My life's journey is... somebody who came from humble beginnings, took advantage of opportunities, and created a better life for the people closest to him. I hope to achieve letting God in me shine through the things that I do.

Contribution:

What do I consider to be my most important future contribution to the most important people in my life? Bringing others to Christ, build generational wealth, Kids follow their passions, and own businesses that will thrive after I'm gone

Talents: My natural talents and fits are: Coach others, build business cases, & analyze big data

Performance:

- I am at my best when... Working with smart people, non-ambiguous situations, clear direction
- I am at my worst when... Ambiguous situations, tight leadership, extreme detail oriented projects

Conscience: I need to make the following things a priority: Finishing my book, opening a gym, starting career coaching service

These are the people, and their attributes, that I hope to emulate:

- Sidney/amazing father and businessman
- Tim A/ Great leader and Public Speaker
- Diamond/ Multitasking, Open Emotionally, and Think Strategically

Balance: These are the things that I can do in each dimension of my life to achieve a sense of balance:

- Physical: Workout 4 times/wk. And take Protein after workouts
- Social/Emotional: Call 1 friends/wk. Email daughters monthly
- Mental: Finish a book every 2 weeks
- Spiritual: Finish a devotional daily

Reflect on the mission statement to make choices, set goals, and prioritize. Continue to write and revise to stay on target with your mission.

Chapter 6: Passion/ Skills Matrix

SKILLS: What do you do naturally?	PASSIONS: What do you love to do?							
	Learning New Things	Travel	Collaborative Work	Individual Work	Budgeting	Coaching	Art	Helping Others
Project Management	Product Management, Program Management, Change Management	Consultant- Generalist, Traveling Project Manager	Change Management, Operations Management	Program Management, Inventory Specialist	Balance Sheet Management, Venture Capitalist	Business Development, Employee Relationship Consultant	Marketing Manager, Advertisement Coordinator	Product Management, Business Management
Problem Solving	Operations Management, Consultant- Generalist	Business Consultant	Risk Manager, Campus Recruiter	Engineering, Information Security, Business Consultant	Portfolio Manager, Financial Consultant	Leadership Development, Executive Recruiter, Risk Management Director	Digital Marketing Manager, Mobile App Designer, Architects	General Consultant, Social Responsibility, Customer Service Rep
Attention to Detail	Editor, Writer, Application Development	On Site Auditor, Events Manager	Event Manager, Virtual Assistant	Accounting, Computer Programmer	Financial Management, Investment Banking, Controller	HR- Manager, Tax Consultant, Leadership and Development Trainer	Process Designer, SEO Manager, Graphic Designer, Techical Writers	Real-estate, Product Manager, Help Desk Technician
Talking to Others	Strategic Analyst, Public Relations Specialist, Career Coach	Event Management, Recruitment, International consultant, Foreign Affairs	Consultant, Vendor Management	Sales, Staffing, Recruiting, Customer service	Product Sales, Sales Training	Career Coaching, HR Specialist, Cognitive Behavioral Coach	Social Media Management	Retail Sales, Recruitment, Vendor Management, Financial Advisor
Analyzing Data	IT Technology, Cloud Architect, Application Development	Tech Consultant, Engineering Manager	Change Management, Information Security, Application Management	Accounting, Computer Programmer, Statistician, IT Support	Accounting, Investment Banking, Quantitative Analyst	Technology Trainer, People Analytics, Agile Coach	Tech Design, Web development, Supply Chain Manager	UX Designer, Cybersecurity Specialist, Information Security Analyst
Analyzing Words	Social Media Management, Advertisement, Academic Development	Legal Consultant, Travel Publicist	Legal, Social Media Content Creator	Legal, Audit, Risk, Compliance	Securities Trader, Brokers, Compliance Expert, Financial Law	HR, Legal, Auditor	Brand Management, Illustrator, Copywriter, Editors, Authors	Office Manager, Digital Marketer
Public Speaking	Training Specialist, Career Coach	Business Development, Sales Director, Campus Recruiter	Executive Coach, Career Coach	Sales Specialist, Social Responsibility	Financial Advisor, Sales Specialist	HR, Motivational speaker, Leadership Development, Director	Public Relations, Event Planner	HR Manager, Social Responsibility, Campus Recruiter, Legal
Research	Business Support, Customer Behavior Analyst	International Research	Supply Chain Management, Legal, Information Security	Data Analyst, Research Specialist, Market Research	Business Analyst, Product Analyst, Financial Examiners	Research Coordinator, HR Generalist	Market Researcher, Industrial Designer	Purchasing Manager, Development Director
Design	Social Media Management, UX Designer	Real Estate Property Designer, Creative Director	Strategic Management, Brand Management	Architecture, Product Management, Marketing Manager, Graphic Designer	Product Development, Financial Reporting	Training Development, Corporate Learning	Marketing Manager, Digital Marketing, Film/Video editing, Animators	Product Management, UX Designer

Chapter 9: Sample "Hello Slide"

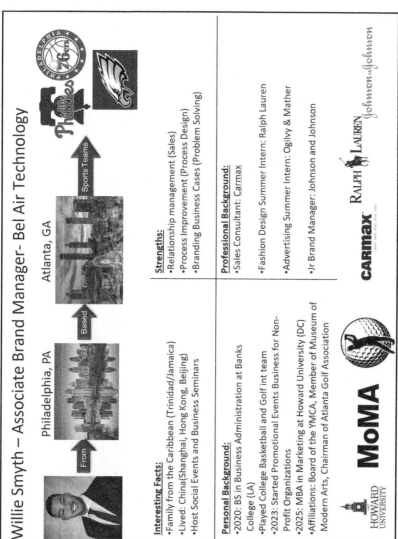

Chapter 10: Sample "Snapshot Slide"

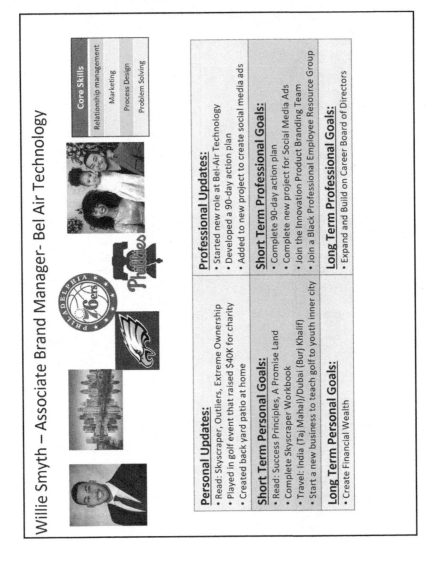

Chapter 11: Sample "Connection Tool"

Name	Contact Information	Role/ Company	Frequency	Personal Facts	Notes
Twopac Shakkur	shakkur@apple.com	Diversity and Inclusion Executive Apple	Bi Annually	Born in Yonkers Has 4 Daughters Plays SemiPro Tennis	3/23/25: Read a book cailled skycraper and recommended it to his whole division 2/19/24: Increase the Diversity 5% in the last quarter. Took his 3rd daugher to daddy daughter dance. Enjoyed a movie called the Juice
Nyomi Campbell	nyomic@gmail.com	Investment Banking Manager USAA	Quarterly	Ran for Government Office in 2012 Recently Moved to LA Owns 2 Vacation Rentals	4/14/24: Purchased season tickets for the Brooklyn Nets. Gave 10K for charity for domestic abuse. 1/27/25: She completed a 5K race. Son got a scholarship to Harvard
Hally Berry	Berryh@hulu.com	Brand Manager Hulu	Bi Annually	2 Sons (Mark and Marc) and 1 Dog (Benji) Loves Country Music	7/27/24: Help increase sales of new product by using a new brand strategy. Started swimming class. Thinking about getting a second Dog.
Tom Hank	TomHank1999@gmail.com	Human Resource Executive Visa	Quarterly	Daughter owns a photography company Has MBA from Cornell Lives in DC	1/30/25: Stated a new project to increase compensation across 3 divisions. 7/30/23: Volunteers for a race in Chicago and had got approved funding for compensation intative.

Chapter 12: Networking Life Cycle

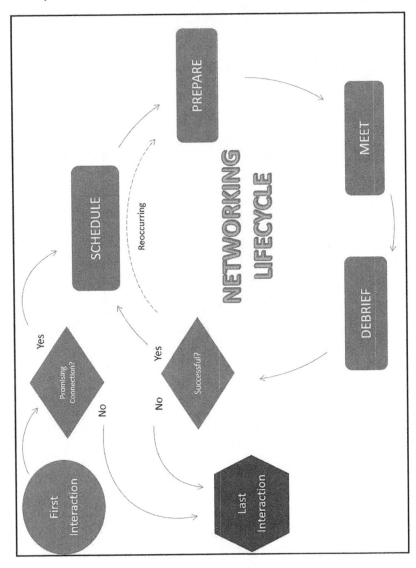

Chapter 13: Sample Annual Update

SAMPLE *Happy Holidays*

Personal Highlights
- ✓ Purchased new home in Charlotte, North Carolina
- ✓ Led the Virtual Book Club, with ~50 members
  - ○ Completed **12** books covering topics on improving financial acumen, thinking effectively, measuring happiness, and becoming a successful leader
- ✓ Started a charity organization to raise monetary donations, canned goods, and school supplies for various organizations based in the Charlotte community.

Professional Highlights
- ✓ Completed the development of an Interactive Marketing tool, a communication request aggregator, which interacts with over 200 associates.
- ✓ Developed a you tube advertisement framework, to market technology benefits to young adults. Once approved, ads to be released 2025
- ✓ Mentored 13 summer interns

2025
I plan on building a foundation for leadership opportunities!

Personal Goals
- ✓ Raise over $5,000 in monetary donations, canned goods, clothing, toiletries, and school supplies for charity
- ✓ Complete 12 books that will expand my mind, teach me new skills, and sharpen my current skills
- ✓ Purchase 2 rental properties in Los Angeles

Professional Goals
- ✓ Gain leadership opportunities within the company on marketing projects that high visibility
- ✓ Develop a groundbreaking process improvement for the Branding team
- ✓ Become an active member of an Employee Network outside of my sphere of influence

Again, Happy Holidays and Thank You!!!

Willie Smyth

Chapter 14: Timothy's Book List

There are 10 Sections with 5 Book Recommendations Each. Enjoy!

(1) Be Humble

- ➤ This is the Day: Reclaim your Dream. Ignite your passion. Live your Purpose
    - ○ By Tim Tebow and A.K. Gregory
- ➤ Talking to Strangers: What we should know about the people we don't know
    - ○ By Malcom Gladwell
- ➤ Dare to Lead: Brave Work. Tough Conversations. Whole Hearts
    - ○ By Brenee Brown
- ➤ Let Love have the Last Word
    - ○ By Common
- ➤ Will
    - ○ By Will Smith

(2) Be Inspired

- ➤ Never Finished: Unshackle your mind and win the war within
    - ○ By David Goggins
- ➤ Can't Hurt Me: Master your Mind ad Defy the Odds
    - ○ By David Goggins
- ➤ Extreme Ownership: How U.S. Navy Seals Lead and Win
    - ○ By Jocko Willink and Leif Babin

- Hustle Harder, Hustle Smarter
  - By Curtis "50cent" Jackson
- A Promise Land
  - By Barack Obama

(3) Build Habits

- Atomic Habits: An Easy & Proven Way to build Good habits & Break Bad
  - By James Clear
- Tools of Titans: The Tactics, Routines, and Habits of Billionaires, Icons, and World-Class Performers
  - By Timothy Ferriss
- 7 Habits of Highly Effective People: Powerful Lessons in Personal Change
  - By Stephen R. Covey
- Presence: Bringing your Boldest Self to your Biggest Challenges
  - By Amy Cuddy
- The Power of Habit: Why we do what we do in life and Business
  - By Charles Duhigg

(4) Understand Money

- Rich Dad Poor Dad: What the Rich Teach Their Kids about Money That the Poor and Middle Class Do Not!
  - By Robert T. Kiyosaki
- Psychology of Money: Timeless Lessons on Wealth, Greed, and Happiness
  - By Morgan Housel

- The Millionaire Next Door: The Surprising Secrets of America's Rich
  - By Cotty Smith and Thomas J. Stanley
- Think and Grow Rich
  - By Napoleon Hill
- Rich Dads' Guide to investing: What the Rich Invest in that the Poor and Middle Class Do Not!
  - By Robert T. Kiyosaki

(5) Think Right

- The subtle art of not giving a F*ck: A Counterintuitive Approach to Living a Good Life
  - By Mark Manson
- Soundtracks: The Surprising Solution to Overthinking
  - By Job Acuff
- Everything is F*cked: A Book About Hope
  - By Mark Manson
- Blink: The Power of Thinking Without Thinking
  - By Malcom Gladwell
- The War of Art
  - By Steven Pressfeild

(6) Think Success

- Mindset: The New Psychology of Success
  - By Carol S. Dweck
- The Willpower Instinct: How Self-Control Works, Why It Matters, And What You can do to get more of it
  - By Kelly McGonigal
- 4 Hour Work Week: Escape 9-5, Live Anywhere, and Join the New Rich
  - By Timothy Ferriss

➤ Outliers: The Story of Success
  ○ By Malcom Gladwell
➤ The Four Agreements
  ○ By Don Miguel Ruiz

(7) Know the Facts

➤ Pay Matters: The Art and Science of Employee Compensation
  ○ By David Weaver
➤ Moonwalking with Einstein: The Art and Science of Remembering Everything
  ○ By Joshua Foer
➤ 4 Hour Body: An Uncommon Guide to Rapid Fat-Loss, Incredible Sex, and Becoming Superhuman
  ○ By Timothy Ferriss
➤ The Tipping Point: How Little Things Can Make a Big Difference
  ○ By Malcom Gladwell
➤ What color is your Parachute? Your Guide to a Lifetime of Meaningful Work and Career Success
  ○ By Richard N. Bolles and Katharine Brooks EdD

(8) Win Friends

➤ How to talk to anyone about anything: Improve Your Social Skills, Master Small Talk, Connect Effortlessly, and Make Real Friends
  ○ By James W. Williams and Russell Newton
➤ Never Eat Alone: And Other Secrets to Success, One Relationship at a Time
  ○ By Keith Ferrazzi

- Leaders Eat Last: Why Some Teams Pull Together and Other Don't
  - By Simeon Sinek
- How to Win Friends and Influence People
  - By Dale Carnegie
- Becoming
  - By Michele Obama

(9) Build a Business

- Crushing It! How Great Entrepreneurs Build Their Business and Influence- and How You Can, Too
  - By Gary Vaynerchuk
- Good to Great: Why Some Companies Make the Leap... And Others Don't
  - By Jim Collins
- The Everything Store: Jeff Bezos and the Invention of a Global Empire
  - By Brad Stone
- Shoe Dog: A Memoir by the Creator of Nike
  - By Phil Knight
- Steve Jobs
  - By Walter Isaacson

(10) Find Focus

- The Monk Who Sold his Ferrari: A Spiritual Fable About Fulfilling Your Dreams and Reaching Your Destiny
  - By Robin Sharma
- Essentialism: The Disciplined Pursuit of Less
  - By Greg McKeown

- Hyperfocus: How to Be More Productive in a World of Distraction
  - By Chris Bailey
- Think like a monk: Train Your Mind for Peace and Purpose Every Day
  - By Jay Shetty
- The One Thing: The Surprisingly Simple Truth Behind Extraordinary Results
  - By Gary Keller

Acknowledgements

I have officially completed my first book! I am both ecstatic and exhausted! This process is a full mental marathon that I am proud to complete. Making it to the finish line was not easy. There are so many people that have directly and indirectly got me HERE.

This work is a product of career events that I have experienced and witnessed. I am grateful for my mentees and clients, over the past decade, that let me lead them in to be more proactive in their careers. Without their trust in me and courage to act, I would not have been able to see the constant results of my *Skyscraper method.*

I must give God the ultimate thanks. His grace has given me this platform, so I am going to use it until he says otherwise. Without him I would not have the thoughts of career advancements or the opportunities to build my dream career. He is behind the scenes, setting me up for success, to exalt his name.

For the development and production of the book itself I feel a deep sense of gratitude:

- To my wife, Diamond you are my north star, my cheerleader, my rock, my wolverine, and my best friend. I am blessed that you walked into my life, literally, on that hot summer day in Chicago. I love that we get to experience life together, forever.
- To my children, Emerald and Elivia, my daily joy comes from both of you. I am loving each stage of your

development, and I know that each of you will lead fruitful lives.

- To my sister in Heaven, Tamika Angelica, my angel, my first friend/life coach. I know you're watching over me with constant love, insight, and protection. I am honored that I get to follow your steps and become an author.
- To my mother, Sonya May, your devotion to Christ is soaked into my core. You are a constant reminder of how prayer truly works. Thank you for pushing me towards excellence in my early development. Jesus Loves you and I do too!
- To my father, Earl Sr, Thank you for your love and support over the years. I Love that as I get older, we get closer. Tanti Po-po is smiling down on us. Pigeon Point-soon come.
- To my Alpha Reader: Sean Wilson, my yardie brudda. I'm looking forward to seeing your successes (50 by 50). Thank you for taking endless hours to review this book, from the ugly stage to the finished product. Your sacrifice to this book's success is unmatched.
- To my Beta Readers: Akil Bello, Stephanie Shannon, Daniel "DV" Williams, Ezenwayni Abii, and Tiffany Lee. Your straight-up, non-sugar-coated feedback gave me a needed point of view.
- To my core accountability partners: Tyrone Jackson, Sidney Hoff, and Jon Suber. Thank you for pushing me to exceed my goals. Let's keep pushing each other to the next level.
- To my Village, my brothers, Earl Jr, Eric, Dale, Travis, Curt, Ed, Remi, Micah. My S&P lunch crew, Marie,

Bunch, Rasheeda, Sean. The Baines Clan, Howard University MBA, Pilgrim Christian Academy, and Howard Ave Family. Thank you for your limitless support. When times get crazy, you are my inner circle of peace.

- To Loreal Andrews-Fontenette, Thank you for your invaluable editing and production assistance. Thank you for your carefulness in fulfilling your commitment to this book.

- To my countless other supporters over the years. Too Many names to mention. You know who you are. Thank you

- To YOU my reader. I'm thankful you took time with my book. It is an honor that you found value in my work. My goal is that not only your career but also your life improves significantly because of this book.

Timothy's Contact information

website www.careersinaction.com
linkedin www.linkedin.com/in/timothy-nurse/
facebook www.facebook.com/careersinaction
email tsncareers@gmail.com